HMS TIGER A

# HMS TIGER AT BAY

## A Sailor's Memoir 1914-18

VICTOR HAYWARD

WILLIAM KIMBER · LONDON

First published in 1977 by
WILLIAM KIMBER & CO. LIMITED
Godolphin House, 22a Queen Anne's Gate,
London, SW1H 9AE



ISBN 0 7183 0295 8





Photoset in Great Britain by
Specialised Offset Services Limited, Liverpool
and printed in Great Britain by
The Pitman Press, Bath

DEDICATED
to the ROYAL NAVY
Past, Present and Future
Ashore and Afloat

# Contents

# List of Maps

## *The Battle of Jutland*



## *Illustrations in the text*

CHAPTER 1

# HMS Impregnable

'One of the Wooden Walls of Old England'

For forty odd years now I have wanted to write this story, and have collected many notes on the subject during my long voyage home. I am now in peaceful retirement after thirty-one tremendous years spent in the Royal Navy, sailing under the White Ensign.

Many details have by now faded from my memory, and I ask the reader to excuse any inaccuracies that may occur in my narrative. I will try to give a reasonable account of the most momentous times during my early years in the Royal Navy, especially the six years and four months spent in HMS *Tiger,* one of the finest battle cruisers ever built in a British shipyard, sailing with the finest ship's company, and serving under some of the greatest officers that ever walked the planks of a 'Battle Wagon'.

Gone now for ever are the hard hitting Leviathans of the Deep, which are no longer required in this atomic age. Long since have these ships departed, their spirits linked with their Viking ancestors in the Northern mists, their bones – like those of many ships – strewn on the ocean floor, seaweed-covered wrecks to the moving tide.

These ships did such great work mostly in the First World War which I hope to write about.

Why I followed the sea, I could not say. Was it because I learnt to swim at the early age of eight years? Or was it because I belonged to three libraries and read avidly all the great sea stories for boys in those days – Charles Kingsley's *Westward Ho!*, Stevenson's *Treasure Island,* and Marryat's *Midshipman Easy* and suchlike?

My ancestors came from yeoman stock and I am the only Hayward ever to follow the sea.

In the fall of 1912, I met an old school chum of mine, Hylton Ormsby, on Cheltenham Promenade. He had recently joined the Royal Navy and there he stood, monarch of all he surveyed, wearing a huge grin on his jovial features, cap stuck at a rakish angle and bearing the name ribbon HMS *Orion*, one of our latest Dreadnought battleships. He was surrounded by a bevy of admiring young girls, eyes sparkling with excitement, all talking at the same time.

Enough said! And when I was old enough I answered the 'call of the sea', sweeping away my parents' entreaties that the life was too hard for me. Although I had never seen the sea, my mind was made up. Soon the Recruiting Colour Sergeant, Royal Marine Light Infantry, got to work on me and after the usual routine – doctor, education, and a recommendation from the local vicar – I was told I would be accepted.

Then came the great day, and scorning a railway station farewell I embarked for Bristol Recruiting Headquarters. Here I went through the same routine. You see, even in those far-off days, they could afford to take into the Navy only what they considered the best.

Later that day I was given eighteenpence and told that I was in. There I remained the remainder of the day and, having nothing else to do, wandered around the Avonmouth Docks and saw for the first time real ships, frowsy little tramp steamers, one or two larger cargo vessels, and I recall seeing one sailing ship with her canvas all furled. I was very thrilled.

That night they threw me an old blanket and I slept on bare boards at the Recruiting Headquarters.

Next morning, with three Birmingham boys, we took the train for Plymouth. At Dawlish Warren I saw the open sea for the first time, and gazed in wonder at the 'white horses' prancing on the red of the lee shore.

It was now the first week in September 1913. We arrived tired but still excited, and a little afraid – remember, we were very young. I was fifteen years and three months old. At North Road railway station we were met by an elderly second class petty officer from the Training Establishment HMS Impregnable, our future harbour home.

It was quite dark when we reached the old historic landing stage at Mutton Cove. Here we received the first view of our line of training ships, three of the Wooden Walls of Old England moored head to stern, HMS *Impregnable*, HMS *Emerald* and lastly, HMS *Powerful*.

They could be dimly seen, a dark floating mass on the black waters, punch-holed with electric light through their great gun ports.

We stepped into a picket boat, all boat hooks and brass funnels, with a coxswain barking orders. Fussing across the broad waters of the Harbour, we skidded to a full stop, breasting the flooding tide to bump gently alongside the great landing stage.

The I got a rude awakening and the excitement of the day was very much on the wane; I was really frightened. Wham! The officialdom of the Navy clamped down on us with an iron hand. Harsh, barking orders. Boys slung queerly in canvas hammocks, jammed tight like sardines in a tin, and poking their heads over the canvas 'gunnels' whispering questions to us as we crept bent down beneath them. The taking away of all our money, except a shilling, the hurried meal of a huge chunk of brawn, a loaf of bread plus a tin mug or thick cocoa. The issue of bedding of a sort, and still the whispered questions from the hammocked boys above us. It seemed like a fantastic nightmare, then blessed sleep wiped away my tears.

Next morning at the crack of dawn, I was rudely awakened by the raucous voice of some huge petty officer 'calling the hands', and I awoke with a hurried jerk. My day had started with a vengeance. There were more questions, and a last chance to back out and go home. I gritted my teeth and said, 'No.' So now I was really 'in'.

'Kitting up' soon was over, all sorts of clothes filling a great canvas bag; then to my horror my lovely shock of red hair was shorn from me like a lamb's, by a most unsympathetic barber, who seemed to relish his job like a mediaeval torturer and grinned like a gargoyle as he invited me to look in the mirror.

I looked like an old time convict and I remember thinking that my dear mother would never recognise me as I recoiled in horror at my reflection in the glass.

Now my nice indigo blue suit was taken away and I was dressed in a second-hand blue serge sailor suit, far too large for me. I felt that I looked like the village idiot.

Then, following a reasonable dinner, there came the swimming test. Scorning the use of the black oak bathing tray inside the old frigate *Circe*, I plunged into the cold water of the harbour and, plugging away, completed the fifty yards in spite of the drag of the white duck suit which I was wearing to complete the test. I passed out with a 'Very Good' to my credit.

Soon we new entries began to shake down to the training routine – seamanship, gunnery, physical culture, and twice a week we came under the thumb of the 'Goes into Bosun', the schoolmaster, elementary education. I considered it was money for old rope to me. We 2nd class Boys understood that we had a lot to learn, and we were helped by the gift of a new volume of the *Seamanship Manual*. Soon we began to understand what it all meant.

We were now cleaning ship with the older boys, and holystoning decks was the highlight of this daily ablution. We used to have to line up two deep in bare feet and with our trousers rolled up well past the knees each morning at 6 a.m. Then at the order from our instructor, we would collect two sandstone blocks, one for each hand, from the wash deck locker, and kneel in two ranks at the after end of the ship we had been allocated to clean. There on the hard teak decks facing our lord and master, whilst he sanded the decks like an old time seed sower, muttering all the while, 'Tons of bite in this grit, me hearties,' and with the cold salt water hose playing gently on the deck, we would slowly advance, rubbing the square stone blocks on the wet decks to clean away all the previous day's dirt. We would take about an hour to complete the whole of the 'upper floor', and then with hard coarse-haired brooms and the salt water hose turned well on, we would sweep the sand away down the scuppers.

Lastly, with the aid of rope swabs, the decks would be dried.

This job caused many of my classmates, including myself, to get an attack of housemaid's knee; the caps of our limbs were swollen like great billiard balls. Jammed like sardines in a tin, lying in our hammocks in the sick bay, we were soon cured by the fleet surgeon and his sick bay 'Tiffies', and in a matter of a few days were back once more in the ranks of the 'holystoning dab dabs'.

Well do I remember my new friend, Boy Faye, and myself one Sunday in autumn, walking through the lovely lanes of Cornwall to that tranquil village of Cawsands where we had our photographs taken. Our weekly sixpence pocket money, augmented by a postal order, paid for this, plus a bar of chocolate and a bun. Later we posted the photographs on to our doting parents. Yes, well do I remember that Sunday afternoon. It was a happy time in a drab world. We became hilarious as, with linked arms, we sang lustily while walking back through the leafy lanes, brown and gold with the autumn sun making dappled mosaics on the pebbled ground.

On the beach, while waiting for the boat, we threw stones into the water. As usual before entering the boat came the order of 'Off Boots', which was obeyed with alacrity. It was taboo to wear 'Purser's Clogs' on the lily white deck of our Noah's Ark, the *Impregnable*.

We lived below decks in long corridor-like rooms, very airless, and kept company with the resident rats; the rooms were ill lit by electric carbon filament lamps that gave out more heat than light.

We had long wooden tables and stools for messes, and slept in the damp air of the lower and orlop decks, stowed heads and tails in our slung hammocks, and by the time of 'Wakey, wakey,' you could cut your ration of air with a pusser's dirk; the atmosphere smelt like Billingsgate fish market, foulness personified.

Here in these messes we were lorded over by a senior *Arethusa* training ship boy, a Mess catering lad proudly wearing one red stripe on his right jumper sleeve.

The food was good and plentiful, roughly cooked in ancient galleys and served on enamel mess utensils; the cutlery was one piece solid metal. The beverage was sweet tea or 'pusser's' cocoa, according to the type of meal.

Our routine was very strict and rigid. At 5.30 a.m. the harsh raucous voices from the 'wet caverns' of the ship's police and instructors' mouths would be heard 'calling the hands', and would herald another day in our training.

The duty instructor would mount guard over the hammock nettings to see that our 'flea bags' were correctly lashed up within the regulation seven turns of marlin hitch, by means of the rope hammock lashings. Then the said hammocks would be stowed like 'packed pilchards' into these huge shipside cavities, and woe betide any offenders. It would be punishment by 'over the mast head at the double', and off we would go with the agility of a scalded cat.

At 5.40 a.m. hands to cocoa and wash in cold water mess tubs, one tub to each mess, and sixteen boys scrambling to dip in their hands and faces. At 6 p.m. 'hands to fall in for clean ship'.

Then at 7.15 a.m. after 'scrub decks', 'hands to bright work stations'; all brass work on the upper decks, such as stanchions, hatch rails, guns, hand steering wheels, marlin spikes, etc. were cleaned with crude metal polish. Then at 7.45 a.m. 'hands to physical drill', usually over the mast head, and 'Do not be last'. Then double round the upper deck. At 8 a.m. 'hands to breakfast and clean into the rig of the day'.

Breakfast would be always porridge, thick with a large spoon standing to attention in the mess kettle. Then either bacon and 'red lead' (tinned tomatoes), 'Channel swimmers' (kippers), 'Boiled Henfruit' – stale eggs, hard as concrete, old 'Toe Rag', boiled dried fish – all this with lashings of bread and washed down with gallons of tea.

This all brings me to a question of clothes. Every day except Sunday our rig would be a clean 'duck suit', which was the regulation dress, Admiralty orders, 'in the Home Waters, for the use of, drill and work'.

We would do our rifle drill on the upper deck of the *Powerful*, and that winter we nearly froze to death, with the keen north-east wind blowing across the corrugated waters of the Hamoaze. We often stood for long periods at attention, accoutred with the heavy leather gear, the small arms equipment, plus rifle and bayonet used in those far-off days! While the instructors lectured us about the drill on the open, cruel, wind-swept decks, often we were chilled to the bone. The petty officers had the privilege of being dressed in blue serge suits. Our white duck suits blown by the cold wind would shiver with us, like 'white sails full and bye', and more than one boy I saw keel over in a dead faint, to be carted off to the sick bay.

At 8.45 a.m. 'clear up decks', and at 9 a.m. the bugle call divisions; that would be inspection by a staff officer; then we had Prayers, led by the 'sky pilot', followed by one of the famous Naval hymns, such as 'For those in peril on the sea'.

Then 'classes to instructions', practical and theory seamanship by means of excellent models, such as anchors and cables, compass and helm, boat work, oars and sails, navigation, rules of the road at sea, lights and buoy markings, signals, etc.

At least twice a week we would land at the small arms range at Cremyl, for squad drill and firing live ammunition, with short Lee Enfield .303 rifles, and .45 Webley Scott revolvers; both these were difficult weapons to handle and would kick like a mule. That brings to my mind the way 'Clam' Gifford, our prize handy merchant – you know: 'it came off in my hand' – halted the Navy like a stopped clock.

We were at the 200 yards rifle range, and about to fire five rounds at a moving target in ten seconds. He failed to put on the safety catch after loading, and whilst getting down into the prone position, accidentally pulled the trigger. Bang went the short Lee Enfield, shattering the quiet of the autumn morning, and the singing bullet went winging over the sixty foot brick safety wall, and a sotto voice said, 'Clam again'.

The .303 landed amongst the farmer's herd of cows in the next field, and the target markers in the butts heard a bellow of rage and shouted to us, 'Wait for it'.

The range officer said, 'Unload! Lower the red flag, then hoist the All Clear white, and fall the boys in, then take them back to the ship. I have got a battle royal on my hands.'

This had happened before, and as we were lining up, we saw the irate famer, red in the face and bellowing like a bull as he climbed over the five-barred gate, brandishing his country walking stick. The range officer said in a tremulous voice, 'Here comes trouble.' We youngsters shook with merriment at the scene, the tubby farmer wobbling up to the crest-fallen officer, howling blue murder all about his prize cows. We laughed till our beam ends hurt.

We found out later that a really good cow had been shot by the stray missile, and had to be destroyed. Also the Admiralty had to pay for the loss of the animal, and the officer and instructor got a rocket, 'a foul wind up the hawse pipe'.

At 12 a.m. 'hands to dinner' – meat and veg, in some manner or other, with bread and more sweet tea.

At 12.50 p.m. 'clear up decks'.

1 p.m. instructions and physical drill, including box horse and boxing.

At 4 p.m. 'hands to tea' – bread and marg with jam, and with stale shop cakes on Sundays.

At 5 p.m. 'evening quarters', when all hands have to be accounted for, an age-old duty to account for everyone in the ship, to make sure no one has been lost overboard, especially at sea. Now was not the time to relax; it was either school, lectures, or wash clothes.

At 7 p.m., 'hands to supper' – bread and cheese with pickles, or brawn, fish cakes, boiled bacon, etc., and more tea, with the usual great hunks of bread like 'leak stoppers'. Yes, we were well fed. After supper, you could relax, and write letters or with your 'housewife' repair clothes. Later at the end of the day, we would go up on the poop or the forecastle just before we turned in, to look and wave to people in boats on the broad river mouth, and watch the battlements of the clouds drifting past the moon, just to unwind from the busy day.

At 8.45 p.m. 'stand by hammocks', and the chief instructor would take charge of proceedings, standing by the nettings and with his bosum's call, pipe 'hand out, pipe down', and the duty stowers hand out the hammocks to the tired boys, only too pleased to get into their slung beds after another hard day. And at 9 p.m. the duty instructor would see that all boys were turned in, and then order 'Out Lights', and switch off, just leaving the police lights burning, to allow the duty officers and instructors to periodically go the rounds and log that all was well, or otherwise.

Sunday was the only day of recreation, and that was only after dinner; the same routine was adhered to up to 9 a.m., except that everyone cleaned into their best clothes for 'Captain's rounds and inspection'. This, of course, included the whole of the ship's company; this weekly ritual was attended by everyone except duty watchkeepers.

From 9 a.m. we boys would be fallen in at division, standing at ease, dressed in our No 1 suits, and receive 'do's and dont's' of what to do or say if questioned by the Skipper, our 'All Highest'. These Captain's rounds caused many palpitations and misgivings to the officers and petty officers concerned, whether their departments would or would not please our majestic Captain.

He and his retinue of officers and petty officers, with clanking swords, gleaming gold lace and jingling medals, could be heard at least one ship away. The three training 'Wooden Walls' were joined by wooden bridges, and very often in fine weather the Skipper would insist on inspecting all decks on all three ships.

We had a boy in our class who was quite a good cartoonist, and he often poked fun at this Sunday morning inspection with his skilful pen, which later he would pin on our mess deck notice board, causing much laughter with his comic sketches.

After our ranks had been inspected by the Captain and his staff officers, it would be 'hands to rig church', capstan bars mounted on wash deck buckets for all lower deck ratings to sit on, and ward room chairs for officers and their ladies to rest their 'stern sheets'.

Church was always rigged under and off the *Impregnable*'s 1st poop deck, beneath canvas awnings. It was here that many of us boys were confirmed by the Bishop of the Home Fleet, and received our first holy sacrament.

Yes, spiritually and morally we were well watched over. After our usual Sunday currant duff (spotted dog), if the weather was kind it would be shore recreation on the Cremyl side of the Cornish coast, but never the fleshpots of the three towns, Devonport, Stonehouse and Plymouth.

Each class went into the Royal Navy Sailor's Rest in Devonport to have tea at least once with the mother of the Navy, Dame Agnes E. Weston. She and her helpers, with her excellent 1st lieutenant, Miss Wintzs, had for many years taken over the task of welfare workers for the whole of the then huge Navy in the three main naval ports, Portsmouth, Devonport and Chatham. The Admiralty had no department for this valuable work.

She also watched over the welfare of all families, including officers'. Her Sailor's Rest, huge hotel-like buildings, was a real haven of refuge for the sailors while on shore leave, where they could – and still can to this day – for a nominal sum get all meals and a private bedroom, rest and reading rooms, etc., and her own type of homespun religion found much favour with the sailors and their families. Her Sunday night services were often packed.

I might mention she was instrumental in curbing much immorality in the naval towns, by getting the chief of police to clear out the ladies of easy virtue from the houses in the streets around the Naval Barracks. Many cruel things were said at the time of her well-meaning efforts, such as, 'She never had a slash of the pork sword' (meaning frustrated); etc., but her tireless work more than paid off. In 1921 she was the prime mover of the introduction by the Admiralty of the threepence per diem in lieu of the naval rum ration. This new order became quite popular with the married men. It helped to keep them in clothes bought cheaply from the purser's stores.

Late in November 1913, we witnessed the launching of that very famous battleship, HMS *Warspite*, nicknamed during World War Two 'The Old Lady'. She was launched from the battleship slip South Yard, Devonport Dockyard. The weather was fine but with a blustering wind puffing little caps on the green wavelets. We stood beneath that well-known landmark, the Obelisk at Cremyl, a granite structure overlooking the harbour. We boys cheered with excitement, our voices linked with the thousands of spectators, which included all the workmen who were so proud of their craftsmanship in such a wonderful battleship. You will read of some of her deeds in this book. At the end of her days she defied the breaker's yard and the elements for four long years, and lay on and under the rocks off the Cornish coast, eventually giving up the struggle and allowing herself to be towed to her place of execution, the breaker's yard.

This to us boys was a red letter day to see this great, gaily beflagged Leviathan gliding down the slipway and then riding gracefully 'head to wind', being fussed about by squat little tugs all pull and shove. It fired us with enthusiasm to be ploughing the sea in a real man-of-war, a deep water ship.

Our training was now going with a swing and we were beginning to gain confidence in our knowledge. Towards the end of the year we began to be trained in heavy gun drill, 6 inch guns and lesser types, including the old Maxim machine gun. Yes, we were learning fast.

Often I would stand and gaze below the poop deck of *Impregnable* reading that great Naval motto: 'No Difficulty Baffles Great Zeal' emblazoned in great gold letters on the old hand steering wheel. A motto that has helped to promote thousands of officers and men, by tenacity of purpose, resolution, and believing that the world 'can't' is not in the English dictionary.

Now we began to approach our first milestone in our naval career, our first leave, and at Christmas. How happy we felt to be able to go home and bask in the love of proud parents while wearing the uniform of a British Jack Tar! I am still thrilled when I think of it.

For days we were preparing for the great event. We kept pressing our suits and ironing our best blue jean collars by means of a wooden rolling pin and a flat board. There were no electric irons in those days. Then came the great eve of our departure. We stowed away our luggage in the schoolroom.

That night we lay in our hammocks and whispered our plans to one another. Gradually the waves of excitement died away and, one by one, we dropped off to sleep. Morpheus had claimed all his victims.

Long before the crack of dawn we were awake and had lashed up our hammocks and stowed them in the nettings, washed in icy cold water, then taken a hurried breakfast. Then, dressing into our No 1 suits (named 'frocks' in those days), we fell in on the upper deck to receive the do's and don't's from the Ship's Police.

Wildly excited, we caught a special train from Devonport and we were off to Bristol. What a journey! We sang all the way. I had wired my parents that I was arriving on so-and-so train, and the family all turned up to meet me. It was like a civic reception. I danced the hornpipe on the platform and we had a whale of a time there and then.

What a leave! I was the apple of all the servant girls' eyes in our neighbourhood. Honestly, they thought I was a real sailor man, instead of a second class 'dab dab'.

My short leave went very quickly and soon I had to say farewell to all my friends and relations. Little did I dream what was in store for me before I was to see them all again.

Soon we were all back once more on board and we got down to our lessons in earnest, knowing that the best of us would soon be selected for sea-going training. The instructors may have seemed harsh but later we all realised that it was for our own good. We were learning fast and in those days it was reckoned that it took seven years to train a good able seaman. Probably that was true, because there was such a heterogeneous collection of ships, old and new, and of all types, steam and sail, serving under the White Ensign.

I remember one incident at this time: the arrival home of the scout HMS *Foresight* from a long commission on the China Station. It was a grey January morning, with a heavy mist hanging over the water. Our Marine Band was up on the poop to welcome them home, playing that stirring sea shanty 'Rolling Home to Merrie England'. We all manned ship, lining the guard rails, and in the inclement weather we cheered those deep water men home after their long sojourn in foreign waters. These real sailor men gladly returned our cheers as their trim, spick and span little craft glided past us to the sound of the 'Still' on the bosun's pipe. We watched her yacht-like figure moving past us, the 'Wooden Walls of Old England', until she was at last swallowed up by the mist of the river.

A few days later we saw the ill-fated *A-7*, one of our early submarines, leave her depot ship HMS *Forth*, with about four hands standing on the forrard casing, dressed in their traditional white woollen jerseys. The little cigar-shaped submarine answered our bugle salute with the shrill whistle of the pipe. It was a lovely morning, her tiny ensign fluttered in the breeze, but alas, that was the last we ever saw of her. Something went wrong out in Whitesand Bay whilst diving, and she sank, to rise no more.

A wave of horror swept round the world at the news. The *Exmouth* sent divers down and they succeeded in getting a wire round her hull, trying to drag her into shallow waters. The hawser slipped and, as time was running out, it was realised that the oxygen in the tiny boat must be also depleted. Slowly, one by one, the entombed men drifted off into the sleep of death.

Outside in the dark green waters, the divers had observed that the reply to their knocking on the hull was getting fainter and fainter until ceasing altogether, and then realised that nothing more could be done to save the lives of the entombed men. The sea had claimed its own, 'The Price of Admiralty'.

By March, there was a vast improvement in our physical appearance; hollow cheeks and chests had filled out and we were glowing with health, clear-eyed and very happy. We could climb the masthead with the agility of monkeys, and up through the 'lubbers' hole and down the other side; we knew our knots and splices, could pull well in a fourteen-oared cutter, and knew quite a bit about sailing. We had learned very much about seamanship and gunnery.

Punishment for offenders was very light extra work or drill, or 'one hour face the paintwork at attention'. I must say our instructors were kindly men; Chief Petty Officers Cook and Padden had sons of their own, and several times when they were Duty Instructors, they would invite two boys to have supper with them in their mess, and afterwards do the chores. I regret that they lost their gallant lives in the action off Coronel, when the *Good Hope* and *Monmouth* were sunk.

The summit of our ambition was at hand. At last the great day came, the first real milestone in our career. There entered Plymouth Sound and anchored off the breakwater, HMS *Gibraltar,* one of the 10th Cruiser Squadron of unprotected cruisers. She arrived with the object of exchanging her 1st Class boys for 2nd Class boys, and to take them away for six months' sea training.

Our harbour training was over.

CHAPTER 2

# HMS Gibraltar – 10th Cruiser Squadron Training.

The Captain of our Harbour Training Establishment gave us a lecture and some very sound advice, as well as a few home truths, and then pointed to the famous naval motto I have previously mentioned. He commended us on the progress of our training.

We said farewell to our very good instructors. They were a splendid lot of chief and petty officers.

So off we went in a harbour tender with our full sea kits, and I personally felt like a modern Columbus setting out on a voyage of discovery, and of course, in a way I was right.

We arrived alongside the old copper-bottomed cruiser, and we all remarked how spick and span she looked. We could see that she had great use as a sea-going training ship. Her armament consisted of two 9·2 inch guns, one forward and one aft, and ten 6 inch guns, five on either beam. Her guns certainly looked menacing, and looking along her upper deck I could see very many smaller guns, six and three-pounder Hoskiss 'Q.F.' Obviously these were her real secondary armament guns. Later I found out that she also had a midship submerged torpedo flat and could fire 14 inch cold torpedoes.

We clambered up her huge ship sides, by means of the great sea gangways, to receive the expected order of 'Off Boots'. These training cruisers were manned by Irish instructors, and they soon got to work on us.

Later, whilst being conducted around the ship with my class mates, I caused much displeasure by walking on a neat figure of eight, a coiled white rope on the forecastle deck. Tubby Verlin, the Captain of the f'c'sle, a great brawny petty officer, built like the leeside of a house, hit me a stinging back-hander and I bounced off the twanging guard rails like a boxer off the ropes. I picked myself up, very crestfallen and hurt, but a sadder and wiser boy.

We had to jump to it and be right smart, everything being done at the double. We were under the iron hand of some of the finest seamanship instructors in the world in sail or steam, and they knew how to knock their knowledge into our thick skulls. We were terrified at their anger and their Irish blood would make their eyes blaze with hate, and we would quail before their temper and punishment. Weather-beaten, horny-fisted, terribly strict, they believed in punishment with the knotted rope's end. But after all these years, I realise that they were also very just men, and in many ways were always looking after our welfare, seeing that we had plenty of food and sleep.

Two days later, we left harbour, bound for Queenstown, Southern Ireland, the base being Harbowline Dockyard, now the headquarters of the Irish Navy. This was our first trip at sea, and what an experience it was!

This 'ocean going crab' rolled like a cross-Channel packet, and when heading into the sea was like a bucking bronco. Soon however we got our sea legs, after a certain amount of sea sickness. We did our sea-going tricks just as if we were able seamen, steering the ship, heaving the lead to take soundings of depth of water, and manned the sea boats, kept lookouts, and so on.

We arrived in harbour and anchored off Spike Island in Queenstown Harbour. Many of the townsfolk came around the ship in their rowing boats to have a look at the new cargo of 2nd Class Boys.

In a very short time we were introduced to the gentle art of coaling ship. This was the hardest and most hated job in the Navy at that time. Attired in our oldest clothes, we climbed down into the holds of the collier tied up alongside the ship, where we made music with our shovels, filling the coal bags. These were winched up on deck and emptied into the ship's bunkers. Very soon we resembled nigger minstrels moving to an orchestra of clanging shovels and whirling derricks. Never had I seen so much coal dust. We lost sight of one another in the swirling black choking clouds. Soon we were coughing like asthmatical old men.

When the work was over, there came the job of cleaning ship. This was a solemn ritual. We manned high powered branch-piped salt water hoses, and with streaming jets of water swept the coal dust over the side. Every part of the upper deck was dealt with, including the masts and funnels, also the ship's side, and of course the wooden teak decks were scrubbed to their usual lily white cleanliness. Then, down below deck, we cleaned everywhere.

Then finally there came the human bodies. Each mess of boys would gather round the communal wooden tub of cold water, and with bars of crude soap would clean the coal dust from our bodies. This of course was done on the upper deck to the hilarious giggles of the young girls in boats watching the naked little sailor boys cleaning themselves. They could see us through the great sea gangways – no modesty here.

Then came the inspection of our naked forms by the Chief Instructor, who was a holy terror. In our turn we would stand before him, legs astride, and then turn about, and if he was satisfied with our general cleanliness then he would swill each boy down with a salt water hose. No doubt about it, cleanliness was a fetish in the Royal Navy – and still is. And rightly so.

Because we were separated from the remainder of the ship's company, we had to live in a very small mess deck abaft the lower gun ports, and next to the ship's galley. Twelve boys to a mess, with the Chief Instructor always hovering around and serving out punishment, a very heavy-handed Victorian type of father to us; we often wished he would 'drop dead'.

The only ray of light in our drab life on board was that the ship's cooks would often give us left-overs of food. There were no bathrooms for anyone except the stokers, so we had at all times to wash, bath and do our 'dirties' on the upper deck.

We often went to sea as part of our training and on one of our trips we did a 6 inch gun night shoot. No moon lit the dark skies but it was clear and the sea was calm. Our gunlayers were dead shots – they had to be, for there was almost nothing in the ship to help them find the target. A tug was towing a battle practice target, and up on the bridge a small and rather inefficient rangefinder suggested that the distance was about 2,000 yards.

But these old time gunnery men had a happy knack of finding the range and spotting their own 'fall of shot'. Some of our boys were stationed on the fore and aft bridge, that is, above and over the top of the guns, and we passed the orders from one to another, and eventually to the crews below. Suddenly a searchlight was switched on and the 24 inch beam eventually found the target. The guns were fitted with electric fire gongs fed from the old-fashioned Le-Clanche cells. It was a thrilling sight to watch the guns being fired, the shells describing a great arc through the night sky, the crescendo of noise, the eerie splitting of the darkness by the belching orange flash from the cordite explosive as the guns thundered out. Soon the target was in ruins, shot through and through.

We found our training much different to the harbour establishment. Of course, it was much more advanced for one thing. We were trained in engine room machinery and stoke-holes, also boiler room work, torpedoes and electrical work of an elementary nature, sailmaking, signal work, and general seamanship. Of course, we also did all the normal work of cleaning and painting ship, but painting with a piece of cloth, for we were not trusted to use brushes in case we lost them over the ship side, especially when working aloft on masts and funnels, or ship sides.

Well do I remember a remark made with great venom by a young leading seaman 'Captain of the Side'. 'I'll make you hang on like flies before I have finished with you.' And in three months that is just what we were doing. We became absolutely fearless when working aloft and none of us came to any harm, except Charlie Burfitt who, while working aloft on the foremast, fell but luckily hit and bounced off the bridge canvas awning, cartwheeling overboard into the sea and breaking a leg.

One day I was selected to deputise for a sick member of the Captain's galley crew, the skipper's boat. This was a great honour. Two days previously I had been promoted to 'Cater Boy', the leading hand of my mess. The galley's crew were under the command of a leading seaman, 'Bungy' Williams. Years later he became well known as a RPO (Regulating Petty Officer).

The boat was long, rakish, six oared, beautifully made 'carvel built' craft painted white enamel inside, dark blue outside, with a thin white line running round the hull close to the gunwhale. All her white silk ropes were kept scrupulously clean. Her two large white sails were made of pure white duck. We kept her woodwork clean by means of 'sharkskin' and salt water. The crew wore special white duck suits, tailor made, plus rubber-soled white canvas shoes.

We worked our oars with clockwork precision when coming alongside any landing stage, the 'Bow and Stern Sheet' men would perform their boat drill like glittering guardsmen on parade. I can see those beautiful long brass headed boat hooks, very white, and the brass burnished like gold flashing in the summer sun. And as the boat moved through the water, the wavelets made music as the oars dipped and flashed with the blades dripping water like teardrops in the rain, from the clean waters of the harbour.

Often we would take our august but genial skipper and his family out to Spike Island for a picnic. I well remember one lovely afternoon in early June. We did just that and our Captain gave the coxswain a gold half sovereign, telling him to take the crew ashore into Queenstown and entertain us, remarking that the steam pinnace would pick him and his family up later. Our gay young coxswain's idea of a good time was to take us all round the pubs, the 'porter houses' along the waterfront, while introducing us to the Irish colleens.

Bungy Williams would slap their 'stern sheets' and say in his soft burring West Country voice, 'Me luvvly darlings,' kiss them and murmur, 'Cheeks like the blush of dawn, and bodies like a Devon dairy maid.'

Luckily I did not drink any of the noxious black beverage. Believe me, when eight o'clock came, the 'swain and most of the boys were in a merry condition and had to be smuggled back on board. How we ever got the boat back to the ship was a miracle.

Now and then our skipper would take part in sailing races against the Captains of other ships in the Squadron, HM ships *Hawke, Endymion, Grafton, Royal Arthur* and *Crescent*. These races were very thrilling events for us boys, being close hauled to a cracking breeze with the green seas rushing past us and spilling over the lee gunwhale in minute cascades. Often we raced our 'Blue Swan' to victory, and to us this was the Sport of Kings. Our Captain was a fine sailing master and knew every trick, and would often order us to hang on with the sails taut as a drumskin, and the masts bending to the strain. It was all very thrilling. Yes, our Skipper knew how to take advantage of every puff of wind, and the boat responded to his touch like a thoroughbred.

What little recreation we had we spent on the Island of Ringaskiddy where a bare-footed peasant woman would sell us good meals for a few coppers. Of this peasant woman I could write a whole chapter. She certainly was a woman you would not meet in a day's march — tall, erect, a deep-bosomed woman with a bust like Boadicea. Regal and majestic, with a smile that could launch a thousand ships, and carry a banner at the head of any army, she was not really old, fortyish, I would say. This kindly modern Venus would call out in her bell-like contralto voice, 'Come on, me little 'earties, drink auntie's tea, sweet as bloody nectar, and eat auntie's rock cakes, soft as yer darling 'earts,' and if you had no money you got 'big eats' just the same from Maggie. Our one-and-sixpence weekly pocket money was soon spent.

One reminiscence of Maggie concerns Cock Ennis, the baby of our class. His true age was fourteen tender years; he joined the Navy with the aid of his older brother's birth certificate and his father's (an old 'shellback') blessing. This dramatic incident happened when the Leading Seaman Captain of the Side had for days been tormenting us with harsh and very foul-mouthed words, sneers and lashes with the knotted rope's end.

Ennis said to me in the quiet of our hammocks, 'You'll see! I'll get that bastard one day.'

I replied, 'Be careful, Cock, don't get into too much trouble. He hates your guts.'

That next day we were doing maintenance work on the main mast with the aid of coarse rags and pots of black, oily 'Stockholm' tar. Young Ennis was up aloft in a bosun's chair cleaning down one side of the mast, while I was doing the same on the other side of the mast. Down below and underneath our tormentor was standing and showing off to the Bo'sun, who knowingly was just nodding his head, when Ennis, with a whisper full of venom, said to me, 'This is it.'

Before I could say anything, he whipped his tarpot off its hook and let go, shouting out, 'Look out!'

Bang went the pot and Ennis scored a bull's eye right on top of the 'Killick's' clean cap cover, and down to earth he toppled, stunned by the force and weight of the oily tarpot, which splashed all over our tormentor. The Bo'sun got the backlash.

The viscous liquid spread a dark stain of hate on the clean white deck, a vicious oath came from the officer, and Ennis, now terrified by his deed, in a flash swung out on to the port main ratlings. He leapt over to the main stays, then with the agility of a monkey slid down the taut wire, straight on to the top of the wide bulwarks, then dived clean over the ship's side, cleaving the water with a perfect entry, and just missing the steam pinnace moored to the port boom.

Exclamations of dismay cried out from the many onlookers, and entreaties to the lad to come back had no effect on Ennis. He struck out with the speed of an Olympic swimmer for Spike Island, about a cable's length away.

Maggie working in her baking hut heard the commotion, came out and saw the swimming lad coming towards her. She waded into the sea, reached the now exhausted boy, and plucked him out of the water by his belt, folding him in her motherly arms like a baby. Then she took him into her hut and before the steam pinnace had reached the landing stage, she got the whole story out of the sobbing boy.

A knock on the closed door, and the stern voice of the coxswain demanded the return of the boy. This turned Maggie from a kindly creature to a raging virago; grasping a huge rolling pin she flung open the door. The petty officer quailed before the onslaught of this angry Amazon, and she spat the words at him, 'Go back to yer ship, ye s'alpeen and fetch an orficer and I'll tell 'im wot's all the trouble about.'

He backed away, cursing, and she flung the pin at him, and he turned and ran back to his boat.

By this time, our good Captain knew all about the escape of the boy, and when the coxswain made his report, he turned to the Officer of the Watch and said simply, 'All right, I will deal personally with this matter,' and stepped down into the boat.

Maggie met him at the landing stage, and over a cup of tea in her hut, he heard the full true story from Maggie and the young boy. Our good Captain knew Maggie very well, and trusted her judgment of the whole episode, so he told Ennis, 'The affair on the upper deck I shall treat as an accident, but do not do it again,' and wagging a forefinger at him: 'For leaving the ship without permission, you will have to be punished.'

Young Cock Ennis was at the Defaulters' Table next day, and on the Skipper's advice was sentenced to three days' extra work, which was more than the usual 'spud bashing' in the ship's galley. And so the incident was closed, but I can assure you it taught the leading seaman to watch his step in future, and he became a much chastened man.

Once or twice we roamed the soggy wastes of Bantry Bay but there was no sport to be had whatever. Our sole object in life seemed to be training, ever training.

Then in July, the 1914 Spithead Review of the 1st, 2nd and

Reserve Fleets, which was a yearly event, took place; this was always held at the same time and the same place.

Our trip to the rendezvous was uneventful and it took the best part of three days at eight to ten knots, which was our maximum speed. Well do I remember the Bosun's Mates piping 'Seaboat Crew Up Ashes'. These old ships had no ash ejectors. We had to manhandle the great steel buckets hauling them up from the boiler room and emptying them over the ship's side. Another of the heavy tasks that we boys had to do.

We arrived with the remainder of our squadron and joined up at the very end of the vast long lines of the great British Fleet. Never have I seen so many warships, then anchored the whole length and breadth of the Solent, and beyond Spithead. Every class of ship was there, from the latest super dreadnoughts of the Iron Duke Class, with their six twin turrets of 13.5 inch guns, down to the smallest torpedo boats with their 14 inch torpedo tubes, and a couple of pop guns – Hotchkiss 3-pounders, still used to this day in the Navy as saluting guns.

There never has been before or since such a vast fleet of warships assembled in one place at the same time. Its magnitude made me gasp with amazement. Most of us lads were goggle-eyed with wonderment. These were the days of the mighty battleships with massive armaments, firing their great guns and heavy shells up to ranges of well over 20,000 yards, and these great heavy ships could steam at full speed, at 21 knots for the latest ships.

Then, of course, came Beatty with his splendid battle cruisers, ships carrying eight 13·5 inch or 12 inch guns, and capable of speeds up to thirty odd knots, the 'Cavalry of the Fleet'. And, of course, the latest light cruisers such as the *Arethusa, Phaeton* and Royalist Class of ship, carrying 6 inch guns and capable of steaming at well over thirty knots. They were the scouts of the Fleet.

There were also quite a number of heavy cruisers of the Defence Class, 9·2 inch and 6 inch guns, capable of steaming at 25 knots. Also the town Birmingham class of cruisers, and that splendid county type, the Essex, all very useful ships. Closer towards us I could see the older pre-Dreadnought Class of battleships, the King Edwards and Formidables, with their motley collection of guns, 12 inch, 9.2 inch, 6 inch and the smaller 12-pounder, 6-pounder and 3-pounder guns.

The author

The Grand Fleet at anchor in Scapa Flow, December 1914. HMS *Tiger* is in the fore-front

Ist Battle Cruiser Squadron in the North Sea, 1915 *From left to right: Queen Mary* HMS *Tiger* and the *Princess Royal*

People today will not realise the vastness of the pre-1914 War British Fleet. We had two British fleets abroad, one in the Mediterranean and one in China, and there were quite large squadrons of ships in foreign stations like the West Indies, North and South America, East Indies, South Africa, to say nothing about the small but very important Commonwealth navies of Australia, New Zealand and Canada. In addition, India had a few small ships. Yes, the British and Empire navies had tremendous sea power, and at that time we were called names such as the 'Gunboat Politicians'. The volume of *Janes Fighting Ships 1914* was very much larger than it is today. 'Britain's Sure Shield' was something to be very proud of in those far-off days.

Never shall I forget that night, standing to attention at the Bugle 'Sunset', the notes of music echoing across the summer scene. Thousands of people like myself were staring in wonder as they viewed the vast assemblies of warships. They were doing the trip 'round the Fleet for a bob', and a very good shilling's worth it was. This was the mighty sea power that our great ancestors had handed down to us through the ages. Drake, Raleigh, Frobisher, Anson, Howe and the great Nelson all had a hand in it, and we were awed into silence. The date was 20th July 1914. Little did we in the Fleet know the real significance of this vast assembly. We did not realise that this was a test mobilisation for the whole of the Reserve Fleet and the call up of all reserves.

These very old ships known in those days as the Baltic Fleet had been partly commissioned and had steamed proudly up with their Reserve Fleet crews to take their position at the very end of the great line of ships. Many of these very ancient craft were almost museum pieces. I remember the Majestic Class *Mars, Jupiter*, etc., very queer-looking ships with two funnels abreast, but later when war did come, they came in useful. Some were used for bombarding the German lines, holding positions close to the Belgian coast.

My thoughts turned to our own ship and I felt that I was serving in a very old man-of-war, but the men were a splendid bunch of seamen and marines, with considerable skill and fighting efficiency.

The Royal Marine Artillery at 9.2 inch gun drill were magnificent, all standing well over six feet in height. They would pick up a 150-odd pound shell and hurl it into the gun loader as if of no consequence. Stripped to the waist, they would serve their gun like Nelsonian gunners of a bygone age. Yes, they and the seamen were certainly masters of their trade.

Next day, the King and Queen, George V and Mary, took the salute, passing down the line of ships in the Royal Yacht *Victoria and Albert*. Standing with them were other crowned heads of Europe.

It was a lovely day and just as the Royal Yacht was leaving her moorings, that great pioneer of naval aviation, Commander Samson, took off with his squadron of seven tiny float planes and flew low, skimming the sunlit waters, and down along the lanes of the serried ranks of ships dressed overall, with their bunting flags, and their crews manning the guard rails to cheer ship. We watched with great interest because we too were manning the guard rails, in fact manning ship, and we witnessed one of these frail little planes alight on the water due to engine trouble.

The vast Fleet looked very gay with the coloured flags fluttering in the breeze and all the bluejackets dressed in No. 8s blue jumpers and white duck trousers, wearing their straw hats and looking like overgrown sailor boys of the Edwardian age. And as Their Majesties passed each ship, at a given signal from the Captain on the bridge, we gave three cheers. So the cheers of the great assembly of ships echoed down the great panorama of naval might. The sight of so much sea power raised a good deal of envy in the hearts of the foreign envoys, and left a lasting impression on everyone who saw it.

That night, for a special treat, we were allowed to stay up on deck instead of turning into our hammocks at 8.50 p.m. to witness the lighting up of the Fleet. Our ships did not take any part in this, owing to the fact that we were not fully commissioned with a proper crew.

The night was fine and, looking round, I saw that the whole Fleet was 'blacked out', not a light burning. Away to the west a faint afterglow from sunset could be seen, and high in the heavens a cirrus cloud stretched up into the sky like stairways to the stars. Then suddenly, at a given signal, a solitary rocket soared up into the night. Hundreds of searchlights split the infinity of the heavens and started to flow willy-nilly across the black dome of night.

Criss-crossing and then sweeping down in parallel lines, the beams swept everywhere, then later pointed to the east and then to the west, halting bars of light across the skies, a luminous lustre, crystal clear, then down to the water's edge flood-lighting the ships, and the bands began to play soft music. In fact, it was a perfect *son et lumière*, the ships standing out in wonderful relief. Then suddenly it seemed that a giant hand wiped across the scene and erased the panorama, and darkness fell.

After a few breathless moments, the whole outline of the warships sprang into life as though in fairyland. The Fleet was lit up; thousands of electric lamps gleamed across the nocturnal heavens, and miles and miles of twinkling lights winked like the light of some giant white way, stretching out into the vastness of the summer night. We youngester gazed in amazement, goggle-eyed and breathless with excitement.

The ships remained illuminated for quite a long time, then all lights were switched off and darkness closed once more on the scene, but before our eyes could grow used to it, the great Fleet broke into real gaiety. Thousands of bluejackets manned the torpedo net shelves and lit 'long and short' signal lights of various colours, and whirled them about their heads. This presented a beautiful fantasy of dappling colours which could now be described like a scene from a beautiful background of a Walt Disney film.

At last, came the bombardment of the night skies with fireworks soaring, banging, bursting rockets, with cascading coloured stars lighting the skies, then going streaming down like meteors into the black waters of the Solent. What a night to remember! The summer visitors going 'round the Fleet for a bob' really had their money's worth. Everyone witnessing the Fleet in such a gay mood must have been deeply impressed.

We stayed a short time longer on the upper deck, then at a sharp order went scampering below decks to our hammocks.

Next morning, we manned ship once more, when the German Kaiser's representative, Prince Wilhelm of Prussia (nicknamed 'Little Willie' during the Great War) passed down the lines in the Emperor's Yacht, *Hohenzollern*.

Then after Fleet manoeuvres and exercises, the rest of the assembly of ships dispersed and quietly, unknown to the man in the street, began to take in war stores.

## CHAPTER 3

# Austria Declares War on Serbia 28th July 1914

'Austria declares war on Serbia.' I heard these words read out by a stoker to his chum. We were on our way back to Queenstown and these two stokers had just come off watch, and were talking and reading a newspaper not far from my hammock. As I drifted off to sleep, I wondered what it all meant. You see, we were not allowed any newspapers and knew nothing of the outside world. It was training, ever training; if there was any spare time then we had to write home, and the Chief Instructor would make sure that we did that. He would report to the Captain if our parents did not answer our letters, and the Captain would give the erring parents a 'rocket'.

We arrived back at Queenstown and for a short time things were normal. For two days we visited an indoor swimming bath where the best swimmers were required to do courses laid down by the Royal Life Saving Society. But all of a sudden the storm of war burst upon us. The situation in Europe demanded us to return to Devonport and to be recommissioned for war duties. It meant feverish activity for everyone.

We rigged splinter mats, took in stores, dumped all the woodwork we could get hold of to prevent fires into Harbowline Dockyard. We coaled ship, which included upper deck cargoes of stacked bags. We worked till we dropped in our tracks and slept where we fell. Next morning, feeling very sorry for ourselves, we upped anchor and the whole squadron headed through a swelling sea for our home port. Arriving in Devonport, we went alongside the wall at North Yard and found ourselves hemmed in by all sorts of men-of-war, all preparing for the coming conflict.

The old Chief Instructor was up on the sea gangway to tick us off in his black book, and as he ticked me off he gave me a parting blast: 'You wait till the so-and-so Germans get 'old of you, me bhoy!'

I was currently in his bad books. A few days before one of my mess mates had been washing clothes and had left the tub on the upper deck. As it was I who was the leading hand of the mess, I received a full salvo from Chiefie and he lashed my backside with a stick. He was the only instructor allowed to use this form of punishment. I slid down the sea gangway rope, after dropping my kit into the waiting tender, glad to see the last of the old martinet.

Standing in the tender I gazed up at the old *Gibraltar* and suddenly the memory of that last evening in Queenstown Harbour filled my thoughts. To me and many more of my fellow classmates, this was the last exquisite memory of Dear Maggie, who by her care for us helped to empty our well of loneliness. We felt that someone close at hand really loved us, and it often made life in our drab world worthwhile. It happened that evening before we sailed for our home ports.

Just as the sun was slanting over the Lakes of Killarney, Maggie, well attired in her Sunday best, left the waterfront. All gaiety in the little pubs had ceased that night; their Navy, the 10th Cruiser Squadron, was going to war, and the news had cast much gloom over the port. She was carrying a huge basket when she stepped into her boat, and with her powerful arms pulled her craft away to *Gibraltar*, which was her 'chummy ship'.

Our kindly Captain and his family had always been good to her, recognising her motherly care for the boys. She knew how badly treated we had often been, and had spoken to our Captain about it, but his reply had always been, 'This is the training service and providing my instructors keep to the regulations, I can do nothing about their treatment.' And as I have related, he was a man of a kindly nature and did his best for us.

But to get back to my story. As she drew near to the ship, our Chief Instructor leaning on the bulwarks saw her and shouted down from the starboard sea gangway, 'Begorra! Ye can't come on board, Maggie, we're going to war.'

'Dry up, yer bloody ould bastard,' breathed Maggie, her fiery temper already beginning to rise. There was no love lost between her and our arch-enemy.

She took a deep breath and then the words exploded from her quivering throat: 'Am goin' to say goodbye to me bhoys and you or the Good Lud won't stop me,' and then hooked her boat's painter on to an eye-bolt on the ship side, and carrying a huge basket slung on her arm she went up the sea gangway ladder with the feline agility of a great cat.

'Chiefie' stepped back before the blazing anger on her handsome face, knowing full well that this Amazon could destroy him with one fell blow. Her strength was magnificent.

Many of we boys, after coaling and all the hard work of preparing the ship for war, had just lain down beside the stacked coal bags. The ship's bunkers were full to the brim; we like most of the ship's company were dead beat. I and young Ennis were asleep close to the gangway and Maggie's voice must have filtered through my sleeping mind. I opened my eyes, rather startled, to see her beloved face.

The Officer of the Watch, hearing the commotion, had appeared on the scene and had said, in his very quarterdeck manner, 'Come, come, my good woman.'

Maggie's quick reply lashed him to scorn as she said, facing the two men, 'Doan't yer good woman me! Is this 'ow yet puts my darlin' bhoys to bed?' and she spat venom with these words. Pregnant with fear for our safety she continued, 'And yer goin' to take them out to war 'against them bloody Germans in this ould tub. She'll either sink loik a stone or burn loik Murphy's barn, if them Germans fires a gun at 'er.'

One boy murmured, 'Good old Maggie.'

The Officer of the Watch and 'Chiefie' were by now utterly defeated, and drew back as the dear, sweet woman with great love and compassion knelt beside the weary, sleeping boys and placed cookies alongside their close-cropped heads. To little Ennis, the baby of our class, she cradled him in her arms and for a little while, crooning a Catholic prayer for his safety.

Then standing upright she said to the now chastened officer and 'chiefie', 'Let us say a prayer to the 'Oly Mary for the safety of all they that goes to war in this ould tub,' and she sank to her knees.

Those standing around her did the same, so moved were they with her religious sincerity and her lovely deep contralto voice rose and fell in prayer. Most of us boys now awake were deeply moved.

'Chiefie' asked for her forgiveness before she disappeared down the gangway, and she readily gave it. The OOW held out his hand, a token of forgiveness for the honesty and purpose, and for coming on board without permission.

The last I ever saw of her was with her head thrown back and a now happy smile upon her lovely face, going reluctantly down the sea gangway, her long gold coloured hair waving in the evening breeze like ripe, uncut corn in the harvest field.

Yes, looking back over the years I can truthfully say that Maggie and Agnes Weston were the two great Christian ladies who influenced the lives of the training ship boys. Maggie, uneducated, must have been a genetic throw back from some renegade Irish nun. She was a real practising Christian. God rest her soul.

We arrived at the Royal Naval Barrack Pier, HMS Vivid, but it did not prove particularly vivid to us; it was in fact a depressing place. Built as a cavalry barrack with messrooms above the stables, it was the most austere place in the Navy at that time. I remember hearing stories that some men during the war sleeping in the heavy gun batteries died from exposure during the winter nights, while sleeping on the bare concrete floors. It was a very unfriendly place.

We were here to be drafted to a new ship and soon were told it would be either the new battleship *Benbow,* or John Brown's masterpiece, the new battle cruiser *Tiger*.

For the first few weeks we did manual work of all kinds, helping the crews of the Reserve ships to prepare for war. We were now rated Boys 1st Class.

The date was 2nd August when we arrived in the Barracks and the actual Declaration of War was on the 4th. I do not remember much about it except that I wakened in the night to the sound of far off cheering and wondered what it meant.

I remember listening to a Petty Officer, a 'bit of a wag'. We were down on the parade ground and he was crying out loudly, 'All men that can ride a bike fall in here.' A crowd of matelots scampered away and fell into two deep, expecting a cushy job. Then the PO with a sardonic grin said, 'Orl right, all you mob will coal the *Maggie*.' Off went the crestfallen tars to the old battleship *Magnificent,* to hump in black diamonds.

One night I lay awake in my hammock listening to the mobilising bugle call (one of the action alerts). The notes sounded clearly in that still August night. I turned out and, putting on some clothes, went down to the parade ground to have a look. Peeping round the corner of 'E' Block I saw the parade fitfully lit by the guttering lights of naptha flares, a crowd of men, a motley collection dressed in all sorts of clothes, half uniform and half civilian. These irregular ranks of reservists were being told off for various ships of the old Reserve Fleet lying in the Prince of Wales Basin. I heard many names: *Juno, Ocean*, and many others. I could hear questions and answers. 'What about our kits?' 'What about our papers?' Then the vague answers. Then the shuffling feet of bent, tired men as they moved off to man their ships.

These were hectic days and, as Winston Churchill, then First Lord of the Admiralty, said, 'If these old ships can fire a gun, we will find a use for them.' These were indeed desperate days and every ship that could steam was required.

Germany had so many warships in the 'Outer Seas', and we knew they would and did prey on our Merchant Fleet. Von Spee's Squadron in Chinese waters, *Scharnhorst, Gneisenau*, heavy cruisers with the light cruisers *Emden, Nürnberg,* and *Leipzig,* and the *Königsberg,* in German East Africa. In the West Indies, *Princess Royal* was employed seeking *Dresden* and *Karlsrühe*. This latter ship was destroyed by internal explosion: *Dresden* surrendered. All these ships were eventually sunk, but it meant the use of many ships, including four battle cruisers, the *Indomitable, Australia, Invincible* and *Inflexible*; the last two were the spearhead of Vice-Admiral Sir Doveton Sturdee, who avenged the loss of Rear-Admiral Sir Christopher Cradock's principal ships sunk at the action off Coronel, off the coast of Chile, the *Monmouth* and the *Good Hope*. Sturdee met Von Spee off the Falkland Islands, and after a running fight sank them all except *Dresden,* but she too was cornered, surrendered, and then sunk three months later.

The *Emden*, after a brilliant career as a commerce raider, was destroyed in the Indian Ocean, driven ashore on Cocos Island by the Australian cruiser, HMAS *Sydney*.

In the Mediterranean, Germany had the battle cruiser *Goeben* and the light cruiser *Breslau*. These two ships escaped into Turkish waters and remained bottled up there, except for a brief sortie in 1918, in which the *Breslau* was sunk.

The Admiralty had many headaches and all was not well inside Whitehall; a whispering campaign against that honourable and capable First Sea Lord, Prince Louis of Battenberg was undermining that gentleman's health. It was soon to reach a climax with his resignation. He was replaced by 'Jackie' Fisher, that old warrior and Father of the Navy, then in his seventies.

Just about this time I walked over to have a look at some batteries of the Royal Horse Artillery and spoke to some of the members of the famous 'L' Battery that were to win undying fame at Le Cateau in France, during the Retreat from Mons. History tells us that they fought to the last man and the last gun, covering the infantry in that desperate rear-guard action. I very much admired their very fine roan-coloured gun horses.

Soon all this mobilisation came home to me with a jerk. One Saturday afternoon I was on recreation leave and when I returned, was told that a messenger had chased me all over the barracks, only to find out I was on leave. I was on replacement for a sick man in the *Ocean*, an old battleship leaving for the Mediterranean.

Many years later I met the man who took my place, Paddy O'Brien; he told me in his rich Irish brogue, 'Bejesus, Oi had three ships sunk under me in no taime, my bhoy, the bloody *Ocean*, the *Majestic*, and the so-and-so *Irresistible*.' All old battleships. Such were the fortunes of war and what is sometimes called the luck of the draw.

One Sunday evening I went with some friends of mine to browse around Plymouth Hoe. The greensward was very crowded with Canadian soldiers who were having a shore spell before leaving for France. They had just arrived from Halifax and since I often wondered how many of that fine body of eager young men returned to Canada.

I pointed out to them Drake's statue and they were most interested. I also showed them the spot where the great English seaman played his famous game of bowls before defeating the Spanish Armada.

Looking around the harbour at that time was the scene of great numbers of captured German merchantmen. Captain Buller, HMS *Highflyer*, had just arrived in harbour, having captured a German bullion ship. *Highflyer*, flagship of the 9th Cruiser Squadron, ran her down off Cape Verde Islands. This prize ship eventually served in our Navy as the Submarine Depot Ship HMS *Lucia*.

Here in home waters the first few hours of war brought action. Before the war ultimatum had expired two German minelayers, the *Friedrich der Grosse* and the *Königin Luise* slipped out of Cuxhaven at high speed and laid mines off the English coast; a legitimate piece of bold enterprise, as they laid them while war was being declared. They were intercepted while returning by the light cruiser HMS

*Amphion*, who chased and sank the *Königin Luise*. While returning to Harwich, and with prisoners taken from the water, the *Amphion* exploded one of these mines and sank with a considerable loss of life just off the North Hinder lightship. Some time later the *Amphion's* bugler became my messmate in the *Tiger*. He was very nervous and seldom slept, and when he did sleep it would be with his eyes open.

Well do I remember the first enemy submarine being sunk by HMS *Birmingham* out on patrol in the North Sea. It was a foggy day, and her look-outs heard hammering on the waters. According to German post-war records, the *U-15* had broken down and her engineers under the cover of the fog blanket were hoping to repair the engines whilst lying stopped on the surface, being off the Moray Firth close to the Naval base of Invergordon. They were taking a fearful risk which cost them their lives. After the first shot had been fired by the cruiser's gunlayers, the Germans managed to get way on their boat by means of battery power, but it was of no avail. The British cruiser rammed her with a sickening crunch and the *U-15* rolled over and went under, then came up stern first, then disappeared slowly to her doom fathoms deep off the Scottish coast.

Towards the end of August came that brilliant action in the Heligoland Bight. Our submarines on patrol had noticed that every morning Jerry sent out a patrol of light craft into the Bight. Commodore Keyes, in charge of submarines, considered the idea of trapping this early morning foray of enemy light cruisers and destroyers by using our submarines as bait. The actual attack was left in the capable hands of that brilliant leader of the Harwich Force, Commodore Tyrwhitt. At the last moment, Jellicoe with the Grand Fleet up at Scapa, decided that it might be a good idea for Vice-Admiral Beatty to be there with his battle cruisers, in case of stiffer opposition.

I well remember hearing about this sortie from actual eye witnesses, men who fought there.

Tyrwhitt flew his broad pennant in the *Arethusa*. An eye witness of this action, later to become a messmate of mine, told me that owing to the poor visibility it seemed that from all points of the compass you could see burning, sinking ships, and due to the morning mist there was a great deal of confusion. Ships kept appearing and then disappearing, and in the general melee that followed the action turned very much in our favour. Sir David Beatty, hearing the noise of battle, steered his great ships to the sound of the guns, and the sight that met the battle cruisers seemed very unreal. Ghostly gun flashes, silver streaks of torpedoes gliding through the waters, phantom ships dimly seen, and in the uncertain light, ships continually altering course. Suddenly the German cruiser *Ariadne* ran foul of the *Lion* and Beatty's flagship blew her clean out of the water with a full salvo of 13.5 inch heavies. She disintegrated in one blinding flash.

Many of the German sailors in the water were picked up by our submarines. Our battle cruisers had been fast when closing in for the kill and soon it was all over and our forces withdrew, counting the cost. As the tendrils of morning mist began to dissipate, the destroyers *Lance* and *Laurel* left the scene, their decks crowded with swimmers from the German ships, and soon the rudely shattered waters resumed their normal summer tranquillity.

The results of this action so well conceived by Commodore Keyes was that the Germans lost the *Mainz, Köln* and *Ariadne*, light cruisers, and the German destroyer *V-187*, which sank stern first, her boiler fires going out with a loud hiss as the water engulfed her, and many other German ships were damaged.

Jackie Fisher, when he conceived the idea of battle cruisers, had been right. His dictum was, 'Hit first, hit often, and then go on hitting.' The Germans had trapped themselves, their heavy units being unable to come to help their light cruisers; they could not 'cross the bar' until high water. By that time our forces were well clear and had achieved this great victory. We lost less than fifty killed and wounded, and all our ships were still afloat and able to steam back to harbour. The *Arethusa* and two of our 'L' Class destroyers were however badly hit.

The German Admiralty had received a sharp lesson. They decided to alter their tactics with no more morning patrols unless they were able to be backed up by heavy units.

You will read later why I have mentioned the next incident in the North Sea. We were properly caught bending and lost in the space of less than an hour three old cruisers off the 'Long Forties', close to the 'Broad Fourteens' – the *Hogue, Aboukir* and *Cressy*. The *Aboukir* was the first ship sunk; her Captain thought she had struck a drifting mine and signalled for assistance. The *Hogue* closed in and lowered her boats to pick up survivors, and she too was promptly torpedoed, quickly taking on a severe list. The *Cressy* was fast closing in when the Captain of the *Hogue*, at last fearing that it was a submarine, warned her to leave the scene. It was, however, too late. The German submarine commander of the *U-9* bagged his third sitting duck and she sank like a stone. A fine piece of submarine work. Three ships sunk by three torpedoes from the same submarine in such a short space of time made the world sit up. The submarine had finally come into its own.

It was now early September and the Naval barracks began to empty. Most of the Reserve Fleet had by now been commissioned.

By then there were only the armed liners to be fitted out and to be provided with crews; this was soon done and they did some splendid work during the war.

CHAPTER 4

# HMS Tiger:

*'If Jerry sinks her, I will build a new Tiger out of my own pocket.'* John Brown, handing over the ship to Captain H.B. Pelly RN, accepting ship on behalf of the Admiralty, *Commissioning Ceremony, Clydebank, 3rd October 1914.*

Early in September we were told officially that most of the *Gibraltar* boys would commission the new battle cruiser *Tiger*, fitting out on the Clyde. Due to the fact that many of Beatty's battle cruisers were away on duty in the 'Outer Seas', Jellicoe stressed that the commissioning of *Benbow*, the new battleship, and *Tiger*, the new battle cruiser, should be brought forward as quickly as possible.

Dame Agnes Weston gave the *Benbow* and *Tiger* boys a farewell tea, and some very good advice, promising us that she would not forget us and would send periodically a few copies of her monthly book, *Ashore and Afloat*. This queenly old lady shook hands with every boy and gave us all God's blessing, and when the welcome books came, the boys would say, 'Good old Aggie.'

Now there was tremendous excitement among us lads. At last we felt we would soon be at grips with the enemy. We had special seamanship instructions for the working of big ships and special 6 inch gun drill, already for the great day. Then on 2nd October, we boarded a troop train at the barrack platform and, amid ringing cheers, we were off to war.

Next morning, after a fitful sleep, we arrived about 7.30 a.m. at Glasgow Central, and trooped into a very famous restaurant named Lockhart's, and had sandwiches with unsweetened coffee, black as the ace of spades.

It was a grey morning when we finally arrived at Clydebank. I shall never forget the first sight of this magnificent ship; although she was covered with the grime of the dockyard, I felt a catch in my throat as I said, 'What a wonderful ship!'

I stood gazing at her full length, nearly 700 foot long with a beam of 90ft 6ins. A friend nearby exclaimed, 'What a *Tiger*! Long, lean and hungry!' To us young boys she looked terribly pugnacious with her great powerful guns. We were deeply impressed, for she was the finest ship we had ever seen, and John Brown had said she would be the only one of her class. I now know that she was a ship designed far ahead of her time. Remember this: in her displacement tonnage she was heavier than nearly all of Jellicoe's super-Dreadnoughts; our Commander-in-Chief's flagship, *Iron Duke*, was at Jutland 25,820 tons; *Tiger* was 28,430 tons. For armour, speed and gun power she remained in memory as top of her class until the launching in 1938 of the fast battleship *King George V*, 28 knots, 35,000 tons, 2 Quad turrets, 1 twin turret of 14 inch guns, weight of armour piercing shells about the same weight and explosive power as *Tiger*'s 13.5 inch heavies. The so-called Mighty *Hood* proved to be a while elephant. I am sure *Tiger* was the finest battle cruiser ever built.

That night, at the commissioning ceremony held in Captain H.B. Pelly's quarter deck day cabin, John Brown remarked when signing the papers and handing the ship over: 'If Jerry sinks her, I will build a new *Tiger* out of my own pocket.' He considered her invincible in speed, hard hitting power, and capable of withstanding some very hard knocks. How right he proved. What a ship! Men who built her and men who sailed and fought in her will speak of her with reverence. What was it that Fleet Street wrote about us during the 1914-18 War? 'Beatty's Beautiful Cats *Lion* and *Tiger*.'

She was captained by four very famous officers: H.B. Pelly, Rudolf Bentick, 'Good Alf' to the troops, Derwent Duff, and, at the end of the war, Paddy Boyle, now Admiral of the Fleet Lord Cork and Orrery. They all reached flag rank and that speaks for itself.

We commissioned with over two thousand dockyard workmen still on board; these men were still fitting the ship out and became for a time a nuisance to our crew of 1,350 officers and men. These workmen had orders to work night and day until finished, but we did not finally get rid of all of them until 1918.

I will try and describe the ship. She was the first battle cruiser fitted with 13.5 inch heavy guns firing a shell heavier than the 13.5 inch light, a projectile nearly a ton in weight. She had eight of these guns fitted in four twin turrets, A, B, Q and X. A was mounted forrard and the remainder in succession to X aft on the quarter deck.

Her secondary armament was 6 inch guns, two forrard on the upper deck but closed in armoured casing, and two aft just at the beginning of the quarter deck, then four each side of the ship mounted below as 6 inch battery decks, which also served as mess decks. There were six guns on either side of the ship. She was also the first ship to have high angle 3 inch aircraft guns, one either side abaft B turret and mounted on what was known as the 'Aerial' decks.

The turret guns were controlled by the spotting top mounted high up above the tripod masts, great steel hollow tubes with ladders inside so that in bad weather one could man the various control positions without being exposed to the elements. The 13.5 inch guns were fired by means of the director tower underneath the spotting top, where the director layer and trainer were in an excellent position to see the enemy and by means of Vickers fire control electrical systems could direct the guns on to the target, and fire all guns at the same time.

The rangefinding was obtained by a huge instrument mounted in the great armoured 'Argo' tower; this 24 foot rangefinder was the very latest type. The tower's cylindrical form was a massive affair, mounted on steel rollers and had nearly all round training. It was situated high above and abaft B turret. Also, there was an after control tower, installed above the main after forecastle deck, where an 18 foot rangefinder was installed, and each turret at the after end carried a 12 foot instrument. All these ranges were fed into a mechanical and electrical computer down in the bowels of the ship, known as the Dreyer's Table (named after that brilliant gunnery officer, Admiral Dreyer) abaft B magazine, where all errors were ironed out for range and deflection, drift, speed of enemy, air temperature, temperature of the cordite, humidity, barometric pressure, windage, etc., and the true range and deflection transmitted to the guns by 'Vickers follow the Pointer Electrical Receivers'. The turrets themselves were the very latest worked by hydraulic power for elevating and training; it also worked the huge breech blocks and chain rammers for the great shells; also the loading cages bringing the ammunition up from magazine and shell rooms.

The anti-submarine guns were of Hotchkiss type three- and six-pounders, handy weapons against the thin casings of the submarines of that era. In peace time they were used for saluting purposes. The 6 ins. guns were not the latest but were very efficient; they were mounted close to the ship side, and had an armoured shield protecting them, so that when trained outboard the gunlayer and trainer were well protected from shell fragments and blast from the turret guns.

Well down in the bowels of the ship you came to the torpedo flats firing 21 inch Whitehead torpedoes from submerged tubes, and carried clear of the ship by means of massive bronze bars weighing over a ton. There were four tubes, two in each flat, capable of firing sixteen torpedoes from each flat, with two spare torpedoes, one in each. The torpedo flats were situated one right forward in the bows, and one right aft abaft and clear of X turret magazine. The torpedo control position was situated in the armoured main conning tower, under the fore bridge, where the ship was steered. The lower conning tower was only used for emergencies.

From forrard in the bows one would notice right up on top of the foremast the crow's nest, where the signal man would be the first 'look out' to spot the enemy, and sound the buzzer alarm to the Officer of the Watch many feet below. Then either side of the director tower one would notice the 6 inch port and starboard gun control towers controlling the fire from the secondary armament guns.

Her night fighting equipment was not very efficient; her six 24 inch Clarke Chapman searchlights left a lot to be desired, but this was changed later in the war.

Looking at the upper deck outline, you would notice the great long forecastle, then coming aft abaft B turret the deck continued underneath the Ariel deck and had a great sweep of space known as the after forecastle decks, with the ship's boat deck above the centre, which also carried the three rather squat funnels close together. Still on this deck was mounted Q turret. Walking aft one noticed a steep 10 foot drop with steel ladders on to the quarter deck, on which the after turret X was situated.

All this gave the ship a very graceful outline, especially with the short mainmast used mostly to carry the after end of the great wireless aerials coming from the foremast.

The ship itself had a displacement of 28,430 tons and was driven by Parson Great Triple Expansion turbines geared for tremendous power, and situated in two engine rooms fed by special boilers of a new design. These boilers were fired from many stokeholes, the fuel being coal with emergency oil sprayers to raise steam quickly. The coal bunkers were situated just inside the great armoured belt to give extra protection. Her speed – well, this was rather secret, but doing the 'measured mile' at Greenock after we commissioned, she very easily logged 31.5 knots, and the engineer commander left it at that – well satisfied. He remarked, however, 'I will not tell you what she will do.'

Her whole silhouette was long, lean and rakish, and she moved through the water at night like a great dark phantasmal shadow, low in the sea, with her bump of funnels staring into the night sky.

There were oceans of space for recreation, on the great long forecastle deck and then on to the after deck. I saw during my long stay in the ship almost every game under the sun played – cricket, tennis, lacrosse, soccer, rugby, deck quoits, roller skating, dancing, and even, later in the commission, summer bathing from canvas baths.

Over the 6 inch batteries, the closed-in deck was a fine place for recreation at night and during inclement weather. This ship had almost everything for the age we then lived in – bathrooms, kit lockers, bakeries, libraries, and so on.

Some old sailors will tell you that there are ships that are good and some that are bad, and some ships that have souls. Well, this good ship *Tiger* was a ship in a thousand and she most certainly had a soul – a ship whose name would live forever.

But I must record for all her goodness she was unlucky in some respects; she was a ship that had many fatal accidents occurring in her and a few suicides. To illustrate my point: the first day we commissioned we had our first death. An engine room artificer committed suicide and the next morning, my old shipmate Boy 1st Class Day, coming up from the mess deck half asleep and half dressed at 5.45 a.m. to muster with our hammocks, plunged to his death with a frightful cry that made my heart turn over. He fell down the 60 foot well of an engine room lift, the shaft being empty and unguarded and lit only by the gleam of a 40-watt lamp. The other boys, including myself, were prevented from following him by the cracking order of 'Still' by the Petty Officer in charge. I felt this boy's death very deeply for he and I had been mess mates for a long time. The lift shaft safety arrangements were completed that very day.

We must have lost through accidents the best part of a hundred of our shipmates in the six years and four months I served in her.

Well, we took in a small amount of coal and some stores, did the 'measured mile' outside Greenock, and then we sailed for Devonport. Arriving at the dockyard, we really got down to work. Alongside the coaling wharf we took in 2,500 tons of the best Welsh steaming coal. This was the worst coal ship of the whole war. You see, we were untrained in the art of big ship coaling and most of the men had grown soft with the fleshpots of barrack life. We worked all day and all night until four o'clock in the morning, then the bugle sounded 'Cease Fire', and I saw great hulking men pitch forward on their faces, asleep before they hit the coal heaps in the holds of the collier.

My chum and I crawled out of the collier, where everyone was still resting, and found a warm place to sleep by one of the bases of the after funnel, where a certain amount of heat was coming from the boilers lit for the auxiliary machinery. At half past seven, I awoke gently to find one half of my body very hot and the other very cold – the slight frost had brought me to the surface of sleep. We stumbled down into the collier and had not been missed.

At last our crew finished this, our first real coaling of our ship. Our crew was a motley collection of active servicemen, recalled King's Pardon deserters, 2nd Class Men for Conduct (the hard cases of the day), pensioners, and all classes of Reservists. The officers were almost hand picked and very efficient.

The next two days we filled up with war stores and ammunition, and then said farewell to our home port, no leave being granted, as we sailed for Bantry Bay to calibrate our guns and prepare for war.

Just before we entered harbour, we received a real thrill. It was a moonlit night with a slight sea. Suddenly we were challenged by a cruiser with a flashing Morse code lamp, which created confusion amongst the officers on the bridge, and our reply was the wrong answer. Action Stations was sounded and everyone rushed to their guns. The cruiser skilfully melted beneath the dark shadow of a cloud bank and kept reappearing, both sides hesitating to open fire. Captain Pelly with great restraint managed to make the cruiser understand by means of a plain English signal, giving the name of our ship. I remember she replied that she was HMS — and proved to be one of our Town Class cruisers out on patrol from Queenstown. We could easily have had a torpedo in our guts.

We began to realise that one of our best and most likeable officers was suffering from mental illness. He stalked around the upper deck while in harbour with a brace of Webley Scott revolvers stuck in his service belt, threatening to shoot the villagers who were trying to sell us butter and eggs.

One evening, after a very hard day's work, when tempers were very frayed, we had to hoist a boat, a job normally for one watch; he cleared lower deck, which meant over a thousand hands being used to hoist this fourteen-oared cutter. Twice we hauled away on the falls, i.e. the hoisting ropes, and ran the boat up to the davits, and still he was not satisfied. He ordered us to do the job again. This comic opera affair was suddenly brought to an end. Up in the booms, a great brawny stoker saw his chance, and when the officer in charge of the operation was bellowing out fresh orders, the stoker picked up a wet rope swab used for drying decks and from overhead wrapped the dripping missile around his neck, bringing him down.

I mention this incident because it was the only time I ever saw the *Tiger*'s ship company in a bad temper. We all felt sorry for this very efficient officer because he was invalided out of the ship into hospital. We always remembered him by his once classic remark at Devonport, when we were working desperately around the clock to get the newly commissioned ship ready to go to war. He 'cleared lower deck' everyone aft, on the after forecastle deck, and in a very earnest speech remarked food was only a luxury and sleep was just a privilege. We all thought then that the strain of getting this great battle cruiser and her ship's company welded into a fighting unit was proving too much for him.

We were always out at sea calibrating our guns, large and small. And the primary and secondary armaments crews got down to real training in the very serious work of preparing for war. This drill was tremendously interesting work. I can still remember the pale face of Petty Officer Collins, the gunner's mate for the 6 inch batteries. At all hours, day and night, he would be drumming the drill into us; even to this day, fifty-three years later, I can still repeat the words. We got to know our jobs so well that we could have loaded and fired our guns in our sleep, but we enjoyed it, especially the 6 inch loader drill, a half gun affair, a steel tray with a real breech block, raised on a platform. We had to go through the motions of loading and firing twelve rounds, the shells being real steel practice projectiles and the cartridges round cylinders of wood covered with leather.

The battery officer would time us with a stop watch and deduct seconds for mistakes. We had competitions with other gun crews and I believe the record stood at one minute, ten seconds. This loader drill became a form of sport and all sorts of scratch crews took part – officers, midshipmen, stokers, carpenters, cooks, etc., all for the fun of it.

Very soon we sailed up and round the shores of Scotland, passing the lovely Western Isles with their wonderful varied hues in the splendid autumn sunshine. After an uneventful journey we arrived in the famous harbour of Scapa Flow, the home of the sealion and seal and almost every known sea bird — pelicans, storks, dipchicks, the mallard, puffin, the stormy petrel, kestrel, cormorant and, of course, millions of the scavengers of the sea, the wheeling seagulls.

Yes, Scapa Flow on a moonlit night could be a place of great beauty. I well remember doing a searchlight test in 1919 and standing by that huge rock, The Old Man of Hoy. The moon was full and opalescent, bathing the tiny islands with a silver glow, so that they appeared to float like a huge chandelier. I looked out across the two fleets, German and British, and they were peacefully asleep, just guarded by the solitary twinkling riding lights. I stood and listened and out beyond the headland I could hear the moaning of the wind, and the pounding of the cruel sea against the rocks of the dreaded Pentland Skerries.

I have known Scapa to look very lovely when in a gay mood but mostly it is the greyest and loneliest spot in the world, and in really bad weather would be bitterly cold and dismal, lonely and unfriendly. This was the anchorage selected for Admiral Sir John Jellicoe's magnificent Grand Fleet of battleships and all the great collection of attending craft.

We anchored close to the old '*Donut*' – the *Dreadnought*. She was quite a small battleship but was the original first Dreadnought battleship ever built, the dreamchild of Jackie Fisher, the Admiral who revolutionised the building of modern warships. She was built secretly in twelve months; when the news reached the world it was swiftly realised that all pre-Dreadnought battleships were rendered obsolete.

This ship was small and squat and carried five turrets mounting twin 12 inch guns, three turrets were mounted in the centre and two on either side of the hull. Being mounted in this manner meant that, if required, a great number of full salvos could be fired. Built in 1906, she had a speed of 21 knots and was a great improvement on all previously built ships. She could fire ten rounds together, projectiles of the same calibre at a much longer range. This made the gunnery far more efficient.

Older ships had a hotch-potch collection of weapons, 12 inch, 9.2 inch, 7.5 inch and 6 inch guns, all firing rounds at different times, making it very difficult for the spotting officer to correct the tell-tale fall of shot, and get his guns on to the target. And the time of flight of each of these different calibre shells not being the same, meant even if all fired together as a salvo the shell splashes, or short and over 'straddle', would make range and deflection finding another great problem for the spotting officer. Since the advent of the Dreadnought, the battleship had greatly improved, being able to carry heavier guns, more armour, and had, in addition, more speed.

Of course, the Admiralty under the drive of Lord Fisher, had also built the battle cruiser on the same pattern – Dreadnought cruisers with the hitting power and some of the armour of the battleship, and with the speed to come into action, 'hit hard and retire', before being caught by the enemy battle fleet.

We arrived at Scapa towards the end of October and the submarine scare inside the Flow was still worrying everyone. (Actually, no German submarine ever managed to penetrate the defences during the 1914-18 War.) Every unknown movement on the water, whether caused by a fish or a seal, sent everyone into a panic. Steam was raised, destroyers and picket boats went racing around the harbour, dropping explosive charges. So Jellicoe took the whole Fleet once more around to Lough Swilly until he was sure that the boom defences were foolproof against the U-boat.

Whilst round at Lough Swilly, we learned to manoeuvre with the Fleet; this was good exercise for our senior officers and helped in our shakedown programme.

On 26th October, the 2nd Battle Squadron left their anchorage off Keckna Keal on an inlet off the west coast of Scotland. These ships whilst returning from battle practice did comprise the following ships: *King George V, Ajax, Centurion, Orion, Audacious, Monarch* and *Thunderer*. Suddenly, without warning, *Audacious* struck and exploded a mine; this was one that had been laid by one of Germany's minelayers, of which there were a number operating around our coastal waters. She soon took on a list, and in spite of a strong effort sank before we could get her into shallow water. Luckily there were no casualties.

This was one of the least known episodes of the war, in spite of the fact that she was seen very low in the water and photographed by passengers of the SS *Olympic*. These photographs appeared in the New York papers a few days later.

When we returned to Scapa we were lucky, her place in the Flow being taken by a dummy battleship formerly the SS *Montcalm,* one of the Canadian Pacific Line boats. She became a member of the Admiralty Phantom Fleet which did such good work in both world wars.

We were certainly getting some thrills. I well remember going on board *Iron Duke,* the Commander-in-chief's flagship, that of Admiral Sir John Jellicoe, to be addressed by King George V and Winston Churchill, the First Civil Lord of the Admiralty. There were clean decks between two midship turrets, peace time canvas screens, and outside the snow was gently falling. I remember one part of the King's speech – 'I have great confidence in my Fleet and its officers and men.'

About this time Jellicoe had to release from the Grand Fleet two battle cruisers, the *Invincible* and *Inflexible,* for the annihilation of Von Spee and his squadron off the Falkland Islands. The loss of these two ships away from the Fleet was partly taken up by the return of the *Indomitable* from the Mediterranean, where she had been hunting down the *Goeben* and *Breslau*.

We joined therefore the famous Battle Cruiser Squadron. Vice-Admiral Sir David Beatty flew his flag in *Lion* and the other members of the Squadron were *Queen Mary, Princess Royal, Tiger, New Zealand* and *Indomitable*. We were always at sea and nearly always were 'shaking down' and fast getting battle-worthy. Often we found ourselves up in the Arctic Circle, doing two jobs – patrolling and looking for German raiders, and shooting at a battle practice target. Our ship was always racing at high speed when in dangerous waters to combat the mine and torpedo menace from a prowling U-boat.

Our great bow waves would thrust a mine clear, and it is very doubtful if a submarine captain could have lined his sights up on such a fast-moving target.

We felt the bitter cold very much because at the early period in the war we only had the Service issue of long pants and vests, which were not enough in the sub-zero temperature of the frozen North. I will, however, return to this later.

There, in the waters of these Arctic wastes and at that time of the year, we had very little daylight, but we did see the aurora borealis which swept down in flashing bars. The colours caught us spellbound with their beauty. Its scintillating, lovely radiance left a strong impression on my mind which I can recall to this day. It was some compensation for the cold work of being on the upper deck working about targets. Often we got out the picket boat when the weather was calm enough, to tow a small target, and we at the 6 inch guns would shoot it to bits with subcalibre guns fitted into the barrels of our guns, and firing a small 3-pounder shell to simulate the firing of a full charge. We did this practice by day and by night.

Towards the end of November, we went with our Squadron to Invergordon at the mouth of the Moray Firth on the east coast of Scotland. Here we carried out full calibre firing with the whole Squadron, and we all felt that we were swinging into tune with the remainder of our battle cruisers. We were stationed here to be nearer the east coast of England, to counter any raids by the enemy.

It happened that the very first raid on the east coast towns of England occurred on 3rd November. The Germans, with a fast battle cruiser squadron, swept in from the sea, and under the cover of the northern mists stole past the Dogger Bank, screened by light forces. They bombarded Great Yarmouth, killing women and children. This news angered us very much as we were most anxious to get to grips with the enemy as soon as possible.

At that moment the largest floating dock in the world was berthed at Invergordon. It had been towed thousands of miles from Singapore, a great feat of seamanship. It was, of course, of wonderful use for ships of the Grand Fleet, for minor repairs and cleaning the barnacles off the hulls of ships so that they could maintain their full speed.

CHAPTER 5

# The Dogger Bank Action

## The Sound of the Guns

On 15th December 1914, we rendezvoused with the 1st Battle Squadron, Admiral Sir George Warrender flying his flag in the *King George V*. This was a strong force, the battleships to the north of the Dogger Bank shallows, and the battle cruisers to the south, with Commodore Tyrwhitt coming up from Harwich, scouting to seaward with his light forces.

We sailed in the afternoon of the 14th from Invergordon and rendezvoused just before dawn off the Dogger Bank. Just as Tyrwhitt and his latest class destroyers, the M's, ran into the enemy screen, south of the Shallows, there was a sharp exchange of gunfire and away on the horizon we saw the flashes and heard the light cannonade. The 'Enemy in Sight' signal was received in all ships, and a few moments later the Commodore's flagship *Arethusa* was replying to the enemy fire with her 6 inch guns.

The light was usually poor, mostly due to mist, around that part of the North Sea at that time of the year.

Hipper, the German Admiral, flying his flag in *Seydlitz,* was well to the land side of the Dogger Bank, and we learned later that he had already bombarded Scarborough and West Hartlepool. We thought we had him when he turned for home. He had to come through either the north or the south entrance through the Shallows of the Dogger Bank. A mistaken signal, however, allowed Hipper to slip through the southern channel, but not before Beatty in *Lion* had spotted the top hamper of the enemy battle cruisers sticking up above the swirling mists which were now thickening.

Sir David asked permission to open fire but was refused by Sir George, who told him to wait until he arrived. We in the battle cruiser chased ahead but by this time the visibility had gone down to a few hundred yards and the enemy disappeared into the mist. Our luck ran out just as we deployed for the kill, and in the following game of hide and seek we failed to find them. During the raid on our east coast towns, no military target was hit except for the sinking of one of our gun boats of ancient vintage, and a minesweeper.

Well, that was that, but we all felt that our turn would eventually come. This raid caused quite an outcry in the newspapers; the headlines read: 'What is Our Fleet Doing to Allow This to Happen?' There was only one answer to this problem: Winston Churchill demanded that the battle cruisers be based on Rosyth, to be closer to the east coast towns. Consequently, a few days later, striking topmast, we steamed past May Island and, leaving Inchkeith on our starboard hand, passed under the great Forth Bridge to moor on seven shackles of cable off South Queensferry. This became our base for the remainder of the war.

We got to know the soldiers guarding the Bridge, the Argylls, who would shout down greetings to us whenever we crept under the huge structure, and the exchange of pleasantries made us firm friends with the Tommies.

On 23rd December, we left harbour to gain our first citation on our list of Battle Honours. Leaving our Christmas dinner ashore, we sailed to take part in the Cuxhaven Raid. This was to be our first minor engagement with the enemy.

We left harbour on that fine December afternoon, knowing that something was in the wind, and in the clear light we steamed past the lighthouse on May Island, in single line ahead flanked by our escorting destroyers, with our light cruisers ahead. We must have looked a grand sight to the keepers on the Barren Rock. Soon we turned on our easterly course to rendezvous off the German coast not far from Cuxhaven, steaming around close to land. Later we had the full report of what happened.

It was a daring raid on the Zeppelin Sheds by a small force of Naval seaplanes belonging to the Royal Naval Air Service, dropped over the side by derricks from the first seaplane carrier, the *Engadine*, a converted cross-Channel packet. They flew up and over the waters of River Elbe and the idea was to bomb the Sheds. It did not work out quite like that, for aerial navigation then was very much in its infancy, and only a few of that gallant small force of airmen found the target. The small number of light bombs exploding on the Sheds did not do the desired amount of damage, unfortunately.

H.M.S. "Tiger", Monday

*From* , *To*

| Hours | Patent Log | Distance Run: Miles | Distance Run: Tenths | Standard Compass Courses | Deviation of Standard Compass | Revolutions per minute | Wind: Direction | Wind: Force | Weather | State of the Sea | Height of Barometer At Th[…] |
|---|---|---|---|---|---|---|---|---|---|---|---|
| 1 | | 15 | 0 | NbyE | Nil | 137 | | | | | |
| | | 5 | 0 | " | - | | | | | | |
| 2 | | 10 | 0 | NbyW | " | - | | | | | |
| 3 | | 15 | 0 | " | " | - | | | | | |
| 4 | | 15 | 0 | " | - | - | NW | 2-3 | ocd | 1 | 29[…] |
| | | 7 | 5 | " | | " | | | | | |
| 5 | | 7 | 5 | SbyE | " | var | | | | | |
| | | 7 | 5 | As reqd E | - | - | | | | | |
| 6 | | 7 | 5 | ~~SbW~~ | - | - | | | | | |
| | | | | - | - | - | | | | | |
| 7 | | 15 | 0 | SbyE | - | - | | | | | |
| | | 12 | 5 | " | - | - | | | | | |
| 8 | | 2 | 5 | As reqd | . | . | E | 2 | bc | 1 | 2[…] |
| | | 7 | 5 | - | - | - | | | | | |
| 9 | | 9 | 5 | NbyW | - | 155 | | | | | |
| 10 | | 18 | 0 | " | - | - | | | | | |
| 11 | | 18 | 0 | " | - | - | | | | | |
| 12 | | 18 | 0 | " | - | " | SWbyS | 2-3 | oc | 3 | 2[…] |

Extract from *Tiger*'s Log for 25th January 1915. *Reproduced by courtesy of the Public Records Office.*

the 25th day of January , 1915 .

, or At Sea

| …t of …eter …l …hed …mo- …er | Temperature Air | Wet Bulb | Sea | Position | Latitude | Longitude |
|---|---|---|---|---|---|---|
| | | | | 8.0 a.m. | | – |
| | | | | 8.0 p.m. | | |

REMARKS

A.M.

1.20 - Alt. co. N by W.

| | | | | |
|---|---|---|---|---|
| 6 | 42 | 40 | 45 | 4 — 0 4.27. Alt co. 16 pts. to Starbd. |

5.30. Alt co. 165 gyro. 5.45 Alt. 151 gyro.

7.40. Formed single line ahead Co & speed as reqd. 7.50. Alt co. 8 pts. to Port together.

| | | | | |
|---|---|---|---|---|
| 5 | 43 | 41 | 45 | 8. 0. |

8.30. Alt co. N by W. Speed 18 knots.
Hands empd. as reqd.

11.40. Held divine service
Buried bodies of
- Arthur Matthews A.B.
- John A Ough Sto. 2/c
- Geo. H. Couch Sto 1/c
- Thos Bradshaw
- W. J. Barnett Canteen Server

| | | | | |
|---|---|---|---|---|
| 71 | 46 | 44 | 46 | Noon |

Some of these heroes were made prisoners of war, some lost their lives, and a few of them succeeded in getting back to their parent ship. We cruised around the seaplane carrier protecting her whilst this operation was going on.

We were thrilled when Jerry sent up one of these Zeppelins, the first we had ever seen. The great dirigible just cruised above us while we blazed away with our 3 inch high angle guns. The *Lion* fired shrapnel shells from her 'A' turret, but the Zeppelin just disdainfully lifted up her nose and cruised away. We were firing short by at least a mile.

Now we had to get home again. Already we had risked interference by heavy units of the German Fleet, unknown minefields, and the added danger of being torpedoed by a prowling U-boat. This was a time pregnant with fear. We were so close to Germany that extra look-outs had to be posted to watch for the tell-tale tracks of U-boat torpedoes. Luckily the secrets of the raid were well kept and we were not attacked.

It took us nearly four days to get back to Rosyth. We encountered the worst storm of the whole war on the way. Great waves tore at us and it seemed that the titanic fury would smash our massive bows in. At times the forepart of the ship would be completely submerged up to the guns of A turret, the lower bridge and superstructure being lost to view under water. Forrard in the ship's company's 'heads' below the forecastle, great steel supporting stanchions were bent and twisted like S-hooks. With a cruel snatch the angry waves tore at our upper deck fittings and as we crawled up the sides of mountainous seas, we fell sixty feet down the green well with a sickening crash, and our guts tore at our heart-strings and bruised our bodies.

No one was allowed up on deck and the second afternoon I had the watch up on the bridge as a messenger. I went up through the main mast to get to the compass platform, but once there I was speedily wet through to the skin, with the bitterly cold spray being thrown up by the gigantic seas.

I remember looking aft along the upper deck and witnessing the screen derricks broken adrift from their lashings and swinging to and fro like a maestro's baton, crashing up against the steel screens with a sickening metallic noise.

Never shall I forget that storm. The wind tore at us, shrieking a demoniac hate and wailing like the sound of lost souls in hell. The few small boats we had were soon swept overboard, their lashings breaking like pieces of string, and most of the guard rails were bent over as though they were made of tin. The noise through the rigging made storm music, which was terrifying with its intensity. Our great ship with its 32,000 tons displacement was hurled about like a cockleshell. We just had to heave to and ride out the storm in the end.

I remember coming off watch, taking a last look at the mountainous seas and watching our bows 'shipping it green', then stumbling down the steel ladder, wet through, and half frozen to death. I arrived at the boys' mess deck and found a scene of utter desolation. Mess tables and stools were floating around in several feet of water, clothes lockers had been wrenched from the bulkheads and were pitching about. What food there was had been completely ruined. The heavy seas tore in through the gunports and ruined everything. My 'ditty box' of personal belongings was swilling around in the scuppers and I could rescue only my mother's photograph. The wooden box was wrecked beyond repair. There was not a solitary soul in sight as I clung to a stanchion and listened. It seemed that the prowling monster from the frozen North was trying to destroy us. I wended my way forrard to the heads, and coming to the sick bay met the sickening smell of chemicals from broken bottles. The scene meeting me was like a battlefield.

The medical staff worked round the clock attending to the victims of the storm, who were lying on the decks, lashed to whatever would hold them. I stumbled my way back to my gun crew and managed to get hold of a ship's biscuit, hard as concrete, and a drink of cold water.

That night, manna came from heaven. Our gunlayer, Billy Lowe, accomplished a miracle and cooked eggs and chips for three of us: Sidney Cocking, myself and the good-hearted Billy sat down in his Mess and we really had a good meal. The cold salt water was washing around our feet, but with huge chunks of bread to help down the meal we felt greatly improved in spirits. Thirty-six hours later, we crept into harbour and the next day we enjoyed our Christmas dinner, with the shipwrights and dockyard workers working around the clock to repair the storm damage.

I well remember this storm for one very human incident in my naval career. When the gale was at its height I had the afternoon watch at my emergency station (loading number at 6 inch gun), and the time to 'close up' should have been 12.30 p.m. Our mess deck clock had been rendered *hors de combat* by the smashing seas through the gunports; our timepiece had been snatched off the bulkhead, breaking the 3 inch holding screws like a piece of cotton, to be hurled into the sloshing water, a mass of springs and wheels. Therefore I did not know the time, and the 'call boy' did not pipe 'Emergency Gun Crews to your Station'; he was hanging over the lee guardrails, sick as a dog.

Consequently, I was ten minutes late at my gun. Our gun captain had already reported me 'adrift', and I knew I was on the carpet.

A burly ship's corporal (ship's police) and myself climbed up through the inside of our tubular steel mainmast, and when we stepped on to the forebridge platform to be taken before the huddled figure of the officer of the watch, the fag-end of a huge sea swept like a whiplash through a shattered window on the port side of the bridge. We were instantly soaked to the skin, and my tormentor cursed me roundly and read the charge to the OOW. My lid (cap) had been removed by the sea. 'Commander's report,' muttered the miserable OOW.

When we arrived in harbour I saw 'Togo' Davis, our good commander, and he said, 'Sorry, Hayward, Captain's report.'

I said to myself, 'It's the chopper for me.'

H.B. Pelly, our very good Captain, looked hard at me, a diminutive figure only sixteen years of age, and then said sternly 'No excuse', to my plea that the 'call boy' did not pipe the order below decks. 'According to KRs and AIs, I could order this file of Royal Marines to take you out on to the quarterdeck and shoot you for desertion in the face of the enemy. However, the regulation states "or such other punishment as hereinafter mentioned". So!' and his kindly face broke into a smile and my heart bounded with joy, 'I will forgive you! But do not be late again; six cuts with the cane.' And aside to my divisional officer he said, smiling broadly, 'Hmm, let him keep his trousers on.'

Ten minutes later in the midshipmen's flat I was tied hand and foot across a box horse and received 'six of the best'. I stood the pain, but my pride was humbled to the dust.

The incident I remember about this festive season was the lovely gift we had from the late Princess Royal, then Princess Mary. It was a personal gift to all the fighting men of the forces; a gilt casket full of sweets and cigarettes, with a beautiful scroll message from her to the 'boys', wishing them the very best, etc.

Once again the enemy raided our east coast and once again they got away with it after killing defenceless women and children. We swore that we would have our revenge, but this time they did not have it all their own way, for the cruiser SMS *Yorck* was lost exploding a mine laid by the new fast fleet destroyer HMS *Abdiel*, forty-knotter. This was her first duty with the Grand Fleet.

On Saturday evening, 24th January 1915, the buzz went round the ship like wildfire – 'They're coming out.' Within a few minutes everyone in the ship knew that at last the sands of time were running out for the enemy.

It was a clear cold night and I was on the forecastle helping to cast off a Duncan Class collier tied up alongside us after coaling. She was there as a torpedo protection in case a U-boat did get through the boom defences. By the way, their crew heartily disliked this duty and with bitterness used to say, 'Destroy us first, we have no armour-plated belt to protect us.'

I was just moving aft through the screen door when I heard a terrific twang and a great shout went up. I knew that a wire had parted. The forecastle men were unmooring ship and poor old Bosun Admans caught the striking end of the wire, the 3 inch hawser breaking both his legs. I can see him now, very tall, six feet four inches, very erect, with a sharp-pointed 'Captain Kettle' beard, a very religious man and an old shipmate of mine, being an Instructor Officer on the *Impregnable*.

We carried him off the forecastle on a bamboo stretcher, and that was the last we ever saw of him; his place was taken by Bosun Macarthy.

We steamed all night at twenty-one knots and arrived off the Dogger Bank in the early hours of the morning. The weather was ideal, very rare for this time of the year, and we felt that at last we had caught Jerry at a disadvantage.

The German Admiral Hipper, flying his flag in the *Seydlitz*, was trying a new ruse of attempting to lure us on to a newly laid minefield. Our battle cruiser force consisted of the *Lion,* flying the flag of Vice-Admiral Sir David Beatty, overall commander of the battle cruiser force, *Princess Royal, Tiger, New Zealand* flying the flag of the second-in-command, Rear-Admiral Moore, and *Indomitable* with the 3rd Cruiser Squadron, and an escort of screening destroyers. We knew that that able commander, Commodore Reginald Tyrwhitt, with his Harwich Force, would be there to assist us.

Soon after six a.m. his flagship *Arethusa* reported gun flashes coming up from the south-west, and they were ideally placed to intercept and shadow the enemy. Sir David Beatty with the 'Enemy in Sight' signal before him ordered all ships to go to action stations. We on board *Tiger* had our breakfast brought round to us by the Paymaster and his staff of cooks and bakers, etc. Forming a single line ahead, we worked up to full speed of the Fleet, that is, the slowest ship, the *Indomitable* 25 knots, 1908, our oldest ship.

The Germans were heading for the east coast once again but we sensed that this was only a feint. The weather was perfect and the sun came up out of the Eastern horizon a lovely golden ball, heralding a fine day for the first encounter between the opposing battle cruisers.

Jerry swung around and altered course for home, and was duly reported by our scouting forces. The time was eight bells in the morning watch, and I remembered Sunday morning in a thousand towns and villages in England would be heralded by a single bell calling the faithful to Holy Communion. And I thought on those things.

Hipper now began to realise that he had tempted Providence too far and they increased speed to try and get out of our clutches. But slowly, very slowly, their topmasts began to appear above the horizon; very gradually we were gaining on the enemy. The rangefinders began to get 'cuts' with their great optical lenses on the masts of Hipper's ships.

Beatty waited until the range came down to 20,000 yards before giving the order of battle – *Lion* to fire on *Seydlitz, Princess Royal* to fire on *Moltke, Tiger* to fire on the *Derfflinger,* and the *New Zealand* to do battle with the *Von der Tann. Indomitable,* our last ship in the line, had to fire on the post-Dreadnought armoured cruiser *Blücher.* For Jerry, the sands of time had indeed run out. The tide of events was running in our favour just as remorselessly as the reading on a sundial.

It was not until nine o'clock that battle was joined. This being a stern chase, only our forrard turret guns could engage the enemy. Turrets A and B, Q and X would, of course, not bear. Beatty's

The author on leave in Cheltenham, October 1918

On HMS *Tiger* in 1914. The author is in the front on the extreme right

HMS *Tiger* in action

ranging shots from the *Lion* at 18,500 yards went well and soon four of the ships were firing, the cannonade rolling out like thunder across the still waters. The *Indomitable* was just out of range with her 12 inch guns.

Our communications operator up in the starboard 6 inch gun control tower started to give us a running commentary on the action. The enemy were now firing back at us and their shots were coming quite close. Through the gun ports we saw the great pillars of water leaping up not far away; we all noticed that the spread of their salvos were very wide, the shell bursts being a long distance apart.

Suddenly *Lion* found the range and very nearly blew the *Seydlitz* to Kingdom Come. Her two after turrets were hit by a full salvo of 13.5 inch shells and went up in a holocaust of flame and smoke, the explosion killing outright some one hundred and fifty-odd men. Luckily they were able to flood magazines and prevent the ship from blowing up.

Our friend up in the 6 inch gun control tower was very thrilled. You could hear the excitement in his voice as he described it. 'She's burning like a haystack,' he shouted down to us. The *Seydlitz* staggered on and then recovered her position leading the enemy squadron. These German ships were very stoutly built.

We were very thrilled with our success but our ship's gunnery at that moment was not too good. One of our destroyers, seeing that we were not finding the target, signalled to us a spotting correction and we found our target. The range was constantly being fouled by smoke from ships steaming fast. Our gunlayer and trainer being outside of the ship passed a lot of information to our gun crew from time to time.

Beatty now edged his ships out to starboard to clear the range of the smoke. Our friend up in the gun control tower now told us he could plainly see the enemy ships, and our trainer and gunlayer also got a good view of the enemy, and said our gunnery was good.

Another reason for Beatty's slightly altered course was to defeat the possibility of the enemy dropping mines in their wake.

Suddenly everyone in the control towers realised that the pre-Dreadnought heavy cruiser Supreme Majesty Ship *Blücher,* the oldest ship in the action, was starting to lag behind the German line. Everyone realised that she was doomed. Soon our rear ship *Indomitable* began to hit her fast and often. She was fast lagging astern now, the bright orange flashes of the bursting British shells being plainly seen.) The German lame duck was getting the big stick.

Now the enemy began to hit us. Up in Q turret, the well-drilled crew had been at cannonade with the enemy for some time, and the rhythm of the crews was remarkably good; the shells and cordite cartridges were coming up from the shell rooms and magazines via the loading room, and hoist with regularity to be loaded into the breach. The shells were handled by hydraulic grab and the chain rammer uncoiled with a hiss to ram the great projectiles into the rifling of the guns. The steady gun drill of the crews manning levers, watching electric instruments with grim determination to do their best; the firing of the huge guns, the great steel monsters recoiling to the explosion of the cordite charges, the smooth running out again with the recoil system – suddenly all this was interrupted by a noise like an express train overhead. There was the shattering roar of an explosion, the ship reeling to a direct hit as a German 12 inch shell struck the roof of the turret and rolled the armour back like a piece of canvas. It killed or injured several members of the left gunhouse crew and for a while all was confusion. Then the Captain of the turret and the officer got some of the spare crew up from below, and once again the turret got back into action, with the dead laid on one side and the wounded removed to the dressing station.

The worst hit we received was in the 'Rowton House', a large compartment below the signal bridge, where the tripod mast met the superstructure decks. An 11 inch shell tore through the starboard aerial deck screen to explode inside the compartment. This was the station for the upper deck fire and repair party, under the leadership of an Acting Chief Petty Officer, the Canteen Manager. Having nothing to do, they were all sitting on the deck whiling away their time with a hand of cards.

After the action, I went up to see the damage and found broken bodies, cards and money scattered everywhere. It seemed as if a cyclone had swept through the compartment, and what was left of the ship's Canteen Manager was a shattered arm and hand still clutching the Ace of Spades. Jerry had trumped his trick.

Above the Rowton House on either extreme forrard corner was mounted the port and starboard 6 inch gun control towers. The steel hatchway covers of the starboard one were closed, and all was well. But the port hatchway had been left open and unfortunately the Engineer Captain of the Fleet had been standing astride the open hatchway. His duties lay with all the Squadron engineering; he was acting as a Spotting Officer. Captain Taylor was killed instantly when the shell exploded, split in twain by the awful blast of the explosion. The Control Officer was also seriously wounded but his life was gallantly saved. He was rescued by one of his crew, Boy 1st Class O'Brien. He carried the officer down the shattered ladder, although wounded himself. For this brave action he was awarded the Distinguished Conduct Medal.

The battle now reached its highest crescendo by opposing forces hitting one another with regularity, the noise of the battle rolling across the sunlit waters. A forest of shell splashes surrounded all the ships. The picture was dramatic with its intensity. Gradually we were gaining the upper hand, five ships on our side against their four, leaving out the light craft. The return fire from the *Blücher* was now becoming very spasmodic.

The enemy were more lightly gunned, 12 inch, 11 inch and ten inch, and the *Blücher*, 8 inch and 5.5 inch secondary armament. Our guns were 13.5 inch heavies and lights, 12 inch with 6 inch and 4 inch secondary guns. The *Blücher* began to drop further and further astern of her consorts and when the range came down to 10,000 yards we in the 6 inch batteries opened fire 'Rapid Independent', i.e. there is the target, help yourself. It was a carve up, all the Squadron raining blow after blow on the unfortunate enemy, an avalanche of explosive steel and, like a tired, lame duck, she absorbed this punishment, her speed slowly dropping away.

At first firing common shell we changed to the more deadly lyddite of greater explosive power. Soon our shots were exploding all over the pre-Dreadnought cruiser. So short became the range that we could see our projectiles exploding on the target. Ben Smyth, our trainer, at this dramatic moment stopped the gun following the target, saying, 'It's bloody murder, Bill,' shouting at the gunlayer who was firing, pressing the trigger by means of a hand grip on the handles. Billy Lowe promptly reminded everyone loudly, 'What about the women and children these bastards have murdered?' in his rich Liverpool Irish voice. He was unrelenting and implacable as the gun he laid and fired, and with retribution in the shape of our questing guns, he felt that the bursting of our shells on the *Blücher* was his advocate for the trial of revenge. The battle recommenced without another protest.

We loading numbers were now having a bad time, the gun casement being full of cordite smoke. It was still a stern chase and we were firing on the forward bearings. As the gun fired and recoiled, the breech worker would open the breech to receive another round and, of course, the wind would blow the cordite smoke and fumes back into the casement, blinding and choking the loading numbers who began to drop out. We had no gas masks but had been issued with black crepe bandages for such an occasion, to wear across our mouths and nostrils, but of course these had to be first soaked with water. We had no water and the Captain of the Gun refused to allow us to use the water in the rammer tub. We asked him what to do and he said, 'Urinate on the bloody things.' So that was that. Often I found I had to load two projectiles one after the other, my opposite shell number being in a bad way. The 100 lb shells began to weigh heavy with continued action, especially now that we were being choked with gun smoke.

The *New Zealand* and *Indomitable* had by now dropped a bit astern of us, because we in the more modern battle cruisers were doing 30 knots. By superhuman efforts our lame ducks managed to work up to 28.3 knots. Well done, the 'Black Squad'! The grimy stokers worked like demons to feed the hungry boiler fires.

At our gun our breech worker now changed his tune from, 'You bastards,' to 'You whore sons,' as he slammed the breech loading handle home. The vicar, Our Padre, was highly amused as he listened to these salty words. He was passing through the battery and listened while watching us at battle with the *Blücher*. Later he told this story to a newspaper reporter and it was duly reported in a Sunday rag.

The battered armoured cruiser was now in a bad way and our friend up in the gun control tower said she was on fire fore and aft, and that flames were even shooting out of her riven sides.

Then suddenly the whole victorious course of the action changed. An 'alter course' signal was flying from the *Lion*'s starboard halyards and at the same time Beatty had ordered another to be hoisted – 'Engage the enemy more closely', before the answering pennant, the executive signal was hauled down. The *Seydlitz* had altered course and her midship turret was able to fire. She hit *Lion* with a lucky shot right in the 'bread basket', the port side aft. This explosion slowed *Lion* down to 15 knots and rapidly she began to drop astern of the British line, with her signals still fluttering from either yard arm.

Calling the fast destroyer *Attack* alongside, Beatty and his staff leapt on to the upper deck and ordered full speed ahead. Off they went after the other battle cruisers which were fast disappearing over the horizon.

Rear-Admiral Moore in the *New Zealand* suddenly found himself in charge of the action, with two rather conflicting signals in his hand. He wondered if the 'alter course' signal was a mine or submarine warning, and if the signal 'Engage the enemy more closely' meant the *Blücher*.

He decided to break off the engagement with the main enemy and destroy the stricken *Blücher*. The fifteen minutes lost was sufficient for Beatty to realise that the main action was now over. He did not blame Rear-Admiral Moore but felt bitterly frustrated – victory within his grasp had been snatched away by bad luck. He had wanted, and indeed expected, to sink the lot. His intention had been a 'cutting out' manoeuvre and to get between Hipper and his home base, and with another four hours of daylight to pound them to bits with his superior ships.

Well, we had to finish off *Blücher*. Our gun crews came up on deck to see the end, when her last gun had been shot away. She was now lying well over on her beam, drifting with smoke, flames and water running out of the various holes in her hull. The German eagle ensign still flew from her jack-staff – she had not struck her colours. The main enemy had escaped over the horizon and only a cloud of smoke marked where they had gone. We could go no further because they were by now entering the safety of their own minefields.

The destroyers *Magic* and *Marne* were ordered in to torpedo *Blücher*, which they promptly did. We watched the remainder of her crew climbing down the hull and jumping into the water. Soon she rolled right over and sank with hardly any vortex; the sea had finally claimed its own.

The destroyers closed in and began picking up survivors, and would have rescued all of them, but had hurriedly to leave to join up with their squadron. They left two boats for the remainder of the German crew in the water.

The stricken *Lion* was now a dead duck. Her speed had fallen away to almost nothing, and *Indomitable* was ordered by Beatty to tow his flagship back to Rosyth. So, with a great 8 inch manilla, and chain cable, she slowly took the strain and worked up to five knots. We left her surrounded by destroyers and steamed back into harbour, where we arrived next morning.

Leaning over the bridge, our soldier friends enquired after *Lion* and we told them she would arrive eventually. They gave us a great cheer and waved newspapers at us, saying, 'It's all here.' The Admiralty had rightly claimed a victory and, of course, the British press made it sound like a great triumph. We were talked about as Beatty's famous Battle Cruiser Squadron. With now two famous engagements, plus the two battle cruisers at the victorious Falkland Islands battle, we were really good propaganda for the newspapers and the British public.

The following day the *Lion* came limping in under the Forth Bridge, being still towed by the *Indomitable*, with the famous signal flying from her yard arm: 'Well Done The Black Squadron Of The Indomitable.'

Six weeks later Beatty went on board and congratulated the stokers and presented them with an oak shield with two crossed steel shovels burnished and polished to the brightness of silver, with the famous signal emblazoned in gold letters around the perimeter.

To return to the events of the time, however. We cheered her in and followed her into the dockyard, still cheering by means of anything that would float – drifters, picket boats, cutters, etc. – our tremendous cheers could be heard as far away as North and South Queensferry.

The whole Fleet went wild with enthusiam for our fighting flagship. Two days later, Sir David Beatty had all his boys mustered around No 3 dock at Rosyth, and standing on top of a bollard he addressed us. Even after the passing of all these years I remember most of his famous speech, and several sentences still ring out clear in my mind. Though a megaphone he told us, 'You have won the first round, so now keep on keeping on.' And with a merry smile he quoted a parody of a poem from a Gilbert and Sullivan opera:

There is a beauty in the howling of the blast,
There is fury in the raging of the gale,
There is a terrific outpouring

When the *Lion* starts a-roaring,
And the *Tiger* starts a-lashing of her tail.

Except for *Lion*, there was very little damage done to the Squadron and about a fortnight later we steamed around to Tyne dock, Newcastle, to have fitted a new armoured roof top for 'Q' turret. Here we watched the building of the last of the Queen Elizabeth battleships, the *Barham*.

During this short spell under dockyard repairs, a very amusing incident happened. Shore leave was granted but no general long leave, except for personnel living within a fifty mile radius, which meant I had to stay on board.

We had an able seaman in the forecastle division, a professional burglar who had rejoined the Navy as a 'Recovered Deserter'. Being now a 'second class man' he slid down over the bows by means of a wire hawser, and wended his way into the outskirts of the town. Finding a large house, he decided that this was a like crib to crack, and entered through a back window. He soon discovered to his horror that he had broken into one of the new hospitals for war wounded which were opening all over the country.

In a panic, he hopped through another window, only to find himself crashing through the glass roof of a greenhouse with a loud, shattering crash, sufficient to waken the dead. He was picked up by an elderly male attendant and taken into the nurses, and, wearing naval uniform, and being a crew member of the famous battle cruiser *Tiger*, they believed the yarn he spun them, that he suffered from a bad head and loss of memory brought on by the action with the Germans. They put him straight to bed and treated him as a war wounded hero. Later his kit was landed and sent to the hospital. The kit consisted mostly of rags, including pieces of old iron which he doled out to the nurses as 'souvenirs' of the Battle of the Dogger Bank.

'It's German shell,' he told them in a conspiratorial whisper.

Believe me, that scamp was quite a hero with his plausible tongue. That yarn caused quite a laugh around the Fleet when he returned to the ship and told us the whole story.

Soon we were back at sea again. It was a moonless starlit night, with the sea the colour of pewter, and as a darkened shadow we slipped through the night of calm waters, on passage to Rosyth. All lights above the waterline were blue lamps, no smoking was allowed on the upper deck – we were told that the glowing end of a cigarette could be seen a distance of three miles from upper deck level to a U-boat prowling on the surface.

Upper deck cabins and so on, where full lighting had to be used, had a special 'dead light' ventilator fitted, and a door switch which broke the lighting circuit when the door opened. In the closed-in after forecastle deck a 'slow match' was left burning, a type of rope smouldering to light pipes and cigarettes, and blue electric lamps were used, there and on the seamen's mess deck. Owing to the 6 inch gun ports, so many men crowded into the crew space at night that it was a rather dangerous and eerie experience. Of course, one got accustomed to it, but the poor lighting caused many accidents, and in rough weather the sloshing water would appear on mess decks phosphorescent and weird.

CHAPTER 6

# The Grey North Sea

Now we were often at sea, sweeping the Kattegat or rendezvousing off the Sylt Minefields, German waters; looking for the enemy. Sometime our outposts would catch a brief sight of their light forces and we would all come to the 'ready' and steam very fast, only to find they had escaped to the safety of their own harbours or minefields.

The army on the Western Front was short of ammunition. The shell shortage was very acute. To help, we in the Fleet did our best; we made bags for holding the projectiles, and shell driving band grummits, a rope band to protect the cupranickel, near the base of the shell, which bites into the rifling of the gun barrel.

We were still working in two watches, port and starboard, which meant very little sleep and rest whilst at sea, and early in the war we were not allowed to sit down in case we fell asleep at our guns. To defeat this order, whilst waiting at our action stations, we would hang our black silk scarves around shell hooks on the walls of the casement. We often fell asleep and, hanging on to the bulkheads, managed to remain standing, just waiting for orders.

In harbour and at sea in calm weather I would often visit the closed-in after forecastle recreation deck. Here the scene would remind one of the Monte Carlo gaming tables, but instead of roulette it was the Navy's famous game of Crown and Anchor, played with a painted board and dice on which you placed your bet. Come here in a wheelbarrow and drive away in a Rolls Royce. The croupier would say, 'Two lucky heads and a crown,' as he rattled and then threw the dice from a leather cup with a great flourish, down on to the board. The whole scene was lit by a candle and, with the blue lights overhead and the smokefilled space from pipes and cigarettes, it made the recreation space a weird and garish scene. Sometimes there would be over a hundred pounds placed on the board when one 'firm' would try to break another 'firm' in a bit of friendly rivalry. A sentry would be placed at either end of the deck to warn of the coming of the ship's police, gambling being strictly illegal.

The watchword was 'Blanket!' At the hoarse whispered cry all would be swept away and innocent cards would appear. Yes, during the course of a night hundreds of pounds would change hands, money being not of much worth to the men of the Fleet at that moment. There was no leave in which to spend it, and after the Dogger Bank action, we all knew that we lived dangerously. Many of us did not expect to survive. I never backed my fancy but I often watched, fascinated by the fever of the throw of the dice. Gold coins were fast disappearing, and the 'Bradbury' Bank of England notes were now being more widely used.

In harbour sports were greatly encouraged. We had a famous Naval cutter taken from the old cruiser *Antrim*. I well remember the shipwrights making the boat more raceworthy, sandpapering and spoke-shaving her timbers, then giving her a coat of special paint to make her glide through the water. I recall one very great boat race which caused more interest in the Fleet than the Oxford and Cambridge duel did to the man in the street. This was the *Tiger*'s seamen versus the *Lion*'s stokers. Leading Seaman Lamb was our coxswain, a useful amateur boxer; he was a great character and, with the physical training instructor, trained the crew.

I met Lamb fifteen years later in Miami, Florida, where he was a trainer to our heavyweight champion, Phil Scott, who was eventually beaten by Jack Sharky for the World Heavyweight Title. Lamb could never stay away from the lure of the sawdust ring.

For this titanic struggle, the stakes were quite small, five pounds a 'thawt', that is, on each of the seven seats, but the side stakes ran into thousands of pounds. All the Fleet were gambling on the race, from Sir David down to the humblest 2nd Class Stoker. When one considers that this was in the days when a pound was worth a full twenty shillings, the amount of the stake money can be appreciated.

Great excitement ran through the Fleet. Both crews trained very hard, even being given a special diet. And at sea a special dry puller was made by the shipwrights, in which the oarsmen pulled their oars but, instead of moving a boat, hoisted and lowered weights. The course was marked out by buoys off North Queensferry and down to Rosyth Dockyard and back, a distance of five miles.

Then came the day of the race. All the Fleet lined up behind the starter's boat. We were going to follow the race in anything that would steam – drifters, motor boats, pinnaces, a canteen boat, and several scratch cutters' crews – to help pace the battling oarsmen. Both crews lined up, dressed in shorts and white singlets, mutton-cloth sweat bands round their foreheads, some of them wearing in addition leather wrist straps and rubber gym shoes to get a good grip on the stretchers.

After a bit of jockeying to get the boats in line with starter's buoy, the umpire took a sight to see that both boats were in line, and at the 'Stand by' both crews took up their positions for the initial first and all important strokes, bending aft with eyes on their coxswains. 'Bang' went the pistol and they were off to a cracking pace, dipping well into the flood tide of the Forth. It was arranged to run the race just before slack water, and it was estimated that when rounding the return buoy at Rosyth the water would be at high tide. That would mean a straight run back to the finishing line.

However, it did not work out like that. Both crews were pulling magnificently and at a very fast pace, and coming up to the Rosyth buoy there was nothing in it. They were racing neck and neck, not a bit of daylight between the two boats. Both coxswains were urging their crews to better efforts, Lamb in our boat nearest to us was working himself into a frenzy with words like, 'Come on, you whore-sons, break your bastard backs,' grasping a spare tiller in his hand and threatening to crown anyone who eased up. Then his vitriolic voice would change to a honeyed entreaty, 'Come, my 'earties, just a bit more,' and to the stroke oar after stop-watching the striking rate, he would urge a spurt. More strokes to the minutes!

It was a magnificent race; the two clinker-built boats lighter than 'slushy's duff' were being driven through the now tideless waters by the superbly trained oarsmen, their ash blades bending in powerful parabolic arcs against the pull of the sparkling waters, their muscles standing out on body and limbs rippling beneath their white skins like 'Matthew Walker' knots.

We were shouting ourselves hoarse, the noise being terrific – all the boats' sirens and steam whistles making a boisterous noise. The whole Fleet was going mad. The Admiral was there in his barge with Lady Beatty. Now came the moment of supreme seamanship –

could they race around the return buoy? Both boats together held water with their starboard oars and started to pull around with their port oars. They were almost round when the oars of both boats fouled one another. Pandemonium broke out. Both crews and coxswains cursed one another and then began to belabour one another with their oars. The umpire's boat ran forward and forced its way between the warring crews, and declared the race 'null and void'.

A couple of weeks later the race was re-rowed and the *Lion*'s stokers won by three boat-lengths, and that was that.

One evening at sea in early March 1915, a dramatic incident occurred. Lieutenant-Commander Blagrove (later Admiral in Charge of 1st Battle Squadron, losing his life in the torpedoing of the *Royal Oak* at Scapa Flow in the Second World War), our very valued first lieutenant, suddenly developed acute appendicitis. The movement of the ship made surgery dangerous; our fleet surgeon felt that the operation would be too tricky to undertake. He went up on the bridge and asked our Captain if it would be possible to return to harbour. Captain Pelly signalled *Lion* and the answer came back, 'Proceed into harbour at full speed.' Our skipper turned to the engineer commander and said, 'She is all yours. Show us what she really can do.'

I shall never forget that evening. It was cold and clear. The night air was sharp as splintered ice, moonless with stars twinkling merrily overhead, appearing very close to earth. The buzz went round the ship and everyone off watch took up stations on the upper deck, where they could get a 'lee'. They were going to watch the engineers lift the safety valves and let the *Tiger* do her stuff.

Soon the great battle cruiser began to settle down into the sea, her stern sinking into the black waves as her great quadruple screws began to get a grip on the water. The forty inch supply fans roared greedily as they sucked in the wind to feed the forced draughts with vast volumes of air, to raise the level of steam for the great Parsons' triple expansion geared turbines.

The stokers worked like demons, feeding the great fires; this was a challenge and this was what they always hoped for, to show the world what their engines would do. Stripped to the waist, their black glistening bodies worked in perfect rhythm as they fed the huge fires with the best Welsh steaming coal.

Great sheets of foam-flecked water rose from our bows in a huge 'V' level with the upper deck guard rails. The great speed waves swept past us to be lost in the phosphorescence of the great broad lane of our wake. Throbbing and vibrating like a giant bow-string, she shot like a great black arrow, aiming at the dark and distant horizon, belting on, a huge black phantom of the night. By two bells in the first watch she was exceeding the speed of her measured mile test, and so she sped on, knifing her way to harbour and hospital for our sick shipmate, on her errand of mercy.

The Engineer Captain came up on the bridge, all smiles, and said, 'Hold on to your hats, gentlemen, we are about to break the world record for a battle wagon.'

So the magnificent battle cruiser, this great Ulysses of the sea on her Odyssey of mercy, exceeded her designed speed and the Captain entered in the log '32.5 knots', which was an obvious white lie. The exceeded speed limit was never recorded; the real figure should have been thirty four-something, which as a land speed would be almost the pace of an express train, a knot being 6,080 feet or roughly, a land distance of one and one-third miles.

We gazed and wondered, 'Has this great ship devoured the sea miles to harbour and safety?' and looking out from the lee of the superstructures, we marvelled. 'What a trip!' It was a night and a feat to remember, and the words of Sir David Beatty came back to me: 'The *Tiger*,' he said, 'is the finest battle cruiser ever built,' and he was right.

We remained on deck in the lee for about another hour until we heard the bosun's mate piping 'Special Sea Duty Men Close up at your Stations'. We knew we were entering harbour shortly, and at about seven bells in the first watch we felt the ship ease speed. The throbbing of the great engines died away, the roar of the whirling supply and exhaust fans easing to their normal note. Soon we saw the great black shadow of May Island out on the starboard hand, then past Inchkeith, then the centre span of the Forth Bridge came into sight, looking for all the world like a huge cat in mid-leap as we passed underneath, startling everyone ashore as the great bower-anchors went down and the cable rattled out. Our patient's life was saved.

Over to starboard, aboard *Sheelah*, (Beatty's yacht) we could see that Lady Beatty was still awake, her figure could be seen against the faint glow of her cabin lights, and she must have been wondering why *Tiger* had entered harbour alone.

I remained up on the forecastle after anchoring, talking to a chum. It was one of those nights, silent as the grave except that over on Bo-ness Sands the flooding tide slapped gently on the shore and seemed to sigh the memories of all the world. Later, without speaking, we walked aft, parted and turned in.

It was about this time that we were called upon to do a rather unusual job. We were asked by the Admiral Superintendent of Rosyth Dockyard to dig out the basin. We responded with alacrity and armed with our coaling shovels hundreds of the Fleet men landed. In a couple of days we had dug out thousands of tons of earth to make the huge basin for the docking and repairing of ships. No mechanical shovels or bulldozers in those days! When filled with water, it held a depth of eight fathoms. It was a vast area and we were thanked very much for the speed with which we had tackled the enormous task.

A few days later we once more went up north to Scapa Flow. The submarine scare was still with us and in one corner of Flotta we anchored, keeping day and night watch manning the anti-submarine guns in the after control.

It was still bitterly cold up there at that time of the year, the middle of March. We tried to keep warm by heating 100 lb. round shot to white-hot heat in 'Blackie's' forge and putting them into sand fire buckets. The modern equivalent would be the off peak electric radiators. The heat was released slowly for some hours.

One incident comes to mind. A member of our crew, a Scotsman and a chain smoker, having no matches, kept lighting his 'tickler fags' with ten shillings and pound notes, igniting them on the hot shots. Money was, indeed, no object!

We used to keep watch at the guns with two men awake all the time, one on the voice pipe and one manning a loaded gun. Often we awoke with a covering of snow on our blankets.

We were anchored not far from our 'phantom ship' and we had a good look at our ghost. She had been the steamship *Marion*. With her wooden turrets, guns and superstructures, she looked a real *Tiger* at a distance. Of course, going close as we did one soon saw through the deception. These dummy ships did good work and our phantom eventually went to the Mediterranean. Whilst cruising in the Aegean she was torpedoed and sunk by a German U-boat but fortunately casualties were light.

I have often thought about these dummy warships and it gave one a strange feeling of unreality to see the 'ghost' of one's own ship so near.

Back at Rosyth, sport began to flourish again, with the Grand Fleet Boxing Championships sponsored, I believe, by the National Sporting Club and organised by professional boxers, of whom a number had joined the Fleet, mostly with the rating of petty officer physical training instructor.

Many great battles were waged in the sawdust rings. Well do I remember one great contest for the middleweight championship. One contender was a stoker of our ship, an Irish lad, a very likeable young man. He had set his heart on winning this match, being a very clever and skilful boxer. His opponent was a Marine sergeant who was very strong and believed in brawn rather than skill. He was a man who carried a very heavy punch and he certainly looked rather overweight, being a particularly big man.

The match was held on board the pre-Dreadnought battleship *Hibernia*, on the upper deck. It was a fifteen-round contest and the young stoker did very well in the early rounds, but gradually the heavier punching of the Marine took its toll. The stoker was finally knocked out in the thirteenth round.

Now came the sad part of my story. A few days later we were at sea on the Northern Patrol, and after the first watch the stoker should have bathed and turned in to his hammock. When the hands were called next morning his hammock was found to be prepared for sleeping but had not been used. He was never seen again. At the inquest it was ascertained that he had used the bathroom and he must have gone up on to the upper deck and been lost overboard. The night was calm, being summer, and the verdict was given as accidental drowning by falling overboard. Most of us, however, held the theory that the loss of the boxing match had turned his mind. The last few days after his defeat he had become morose and withdrawn.

Back again in harbour the boys of the Fleet started to compete for the Elgin Cup, a large silver trophy presented by Lord Elgin, whose estate lay in large grounds outside Rosyth. His son was a midshipman on board our ship. This competition was for all types of sport. The most popular was the Marathon Race. I competed for this three times, running the course which was from the dockyard gates to Lord Elgin's estate and right around the grounds, a distance of seven and a half miles. Twice I came in sixth, out of a field of thirty runners. The last time I competed I came in seventh; not too bad, I suppose.

Of course, boat pulling was also a very popular event for the Cup. And many a five-mile race we had in a fourteen-oared cutter. We were extremely fit young men.

There were three Fleet periodicals in circulation at that time: *The Blue Jacket and Soldier* and *Told At One Bell* later both amalgamated into *The Fleet; Ashore and Afloat*, and the Royal Marine paper, *The Globe and Laurel*. These books were of great interest to both officers and men of Jellicoe's Grand Fleet. It kept us in touch with service matters. Mark you, we had our own grapevine and we got to know quite a lot of news passed from hand to mouth by boats' crews, etc. because at this period in the war there was no general recreation leave for the men, except when ships were in dockyard hands.

It was by the 'new' grapevine and the dismissal of our first gunnery officer to a shore job at Sunderland that we knew that Jackie Fisher, the First Sea Lord of the Admiralty, was displeased, because as he put it, 'Beatty's battle cruisers had failed to sink the lot.'

Captain Pelly 'cleared lower deck' and tactfully told us the whole story of the armchair critics at the Admiralty, saying how sorry he was to lose his gunnery officer.

Next day, after the usual morning 6 inch gun drill, Jumper Collins, our battery gunner's mate, said quietly to me, 'Old Fisher found in our gunnery jack a scapegoat.' He then paused and reflectively said to me, 'In years to come, if we live, we shall hear about this again. Historians will shackle on to that old bastard's condemnation of our "gunnery jack". But ignore it – remember this! In the beginning of the action our target was obscured by funnel smoke from our own destroyers, but when Beatty signalled them to alter course to clear the range, we straddled our target and scored several hits visible from the fore top. And remember this! The director trainer is a mess mate of mine and he saw quite a lot, and he is no liar. No, that old bastard [Jackie Fisher] wanted a scape goat and the weakest goes to the wall, and I for one am very sorry to see our good gunnery officer put ashore on the shelf!'

Of course, many popular songs were paraphrased. One of Irving

Berlin's successes, 'You Called me Baby Doll a Year Ago' went like this, I recall:

> We had the morning in the chains,
> Till we got in Paravanes,
> And then 2,000 tons of ruddy coal ...

That, of course, brings me to the burning topic that was always in our minds, that of coaling ship. Everyone in the ship did this hard duty, from the Captain downwards, except the men on watch, and the only people excused were the wireless operators – hoping to keep their ears clear of coal dust.

That brings me to the queer rigs worn by men while preparing for this very dirty task. One young ordinary seaman would enter the hold in the full dress of a German cavalryman which he had taken off a dead German as a souvenir. Like many boys, he had enlisted in the Army but when his real age was discovered – he was then only seventeen – he was sent home. Promptly he re-enlisted in the Navy. There he would stand on top of the coal, in the full dress of a Uhlan, plumed helmet, coloured tunic, striped riding trousers, jackboots, lance and spurs, in fact, the lot!

Another rating would appear in full evening dress; this middle-aged reservist was a wealthy industrialist but, of course, was called up at the outbreak of war, being a Royal Fleet Reservist. There he would appear in frock coat, white tie and tails and, of course, a silk topper. Mark you, however, why these two appeared so spotless and so well attired will always remain a mystery to me. Both characters would time their appearance together; the cavalryman would give a Prussian salute and the gentleman would raise his topper and make a graceful bow, the acme of elegance. It was all very amusing and interesting.

This wealthy industrialist we nicknamed 'The Governor', and I must say he never lost the elegant touch. I well remember passing his mess one morning at breakfast time, when he was the duty cook, and I stood and watched this great character attired in a clean white jacket dishing out the meal, and as he handed out the plates he did say with the voice of a respectful baronial butler, linked with a triumphant smile, 'Your eggs and bacon, sir,' just as if he was handing out the head of John the Baptist.

It was about this time that Jerry tried to bomb the battle cruisers whilst lying at anchor below the Forth Bridge. Their night navigation was poor and they mistook Leith for Rosyth, and away in the distance we heard the beat of their engines. But the noise was receding, so wisely we did not switch on our searchlights, and they missed us, but scored a bull's eye on a whisky storehouse at Leith. Soon the streets were awash with the precious liquid. Jerry's bomb created almost a scene from Dante's *Inferno*. Men, women and kids were out lapping it up, and filling up bottles and jugs. What a carve up! Our canteen manager was fourteen hours adrift from the ship, and on his return and to the officer of the watch's classic question, 'I know! But why?' his reply was, 'You see, sir, it was a pity to see all that stagger juice going to waste. So I joined in with the Jocks and before long I was as drunk as a fiddler's bitch, and my back teeth were awash.'

Calmer days and warmer weather made life far more reasonable, even at sea. Our chummy ship, the *Queen Mary,* taught us how to enjoy life to the full. She would fill up a canvas swimming bath made from peace-time awnings, and kept it full by means of two salt-water hoses running all the while. We could dive in and swim a few strokes, finding it very enjoyable in summer evenings, and we even rigged it at sea when the weather was fine. The bath being underneath Q turret guns, it did not impair the fighting efficiency of the ship.

Some time in July we received a real piece of good news. We were to go to Invergordon and the floating dock, to clean the ship's bottom and overhaul the ship's engines. That, of course, meant that it was our turn for a week's leave. Marvellous! We duly arrived, the dock was pumped out and, singing, laughing and in high spirits, we cleaned the ship's bottom in record time. One party cleaned and the other party painted with anti-fouling.

Then, having changed into our No 1 suits, we boarded the waiting train to take us home for a well-earned seven days' leave. Owing to the war, I had not been home since Christmas 1913. The railway engine would draw us to the 'Mecca of our dreams'; it all seemed too good to be true.

It was a lovely day and the sun was abaft the mast when the wooden-seated carriage train pulled away from the dockside. We gave a mighty cheer for our now famous battle cruiser. Arriving home, I think that half Cheltenham was there to welcome me; even the Station Master wore his silk hat. I had a really wonderful leave but all too soon it was over and I was back on board again. My brief stay in the 'land of the fleshpots' became a remote memory.

Soon we were at sea again with the remainder of our Squadron.

After the heart-breaking tasks of coaling, provisioning and ammunitioning ship, we were glad to rest at our guns, lying on the steel decks.

Accidents were still with us and, arriving back at Rosyth, we had a fatality whilst coaling ships. A swaying, twenty-bag hoist crushed a man against the side of the hold and his life was snuffed out like a candle. A couple of days later, while at sea, two seamen were washed overboard during a sudden alter course due to a submarine alarm. They were wearing the new issue of heavy leather sea boots and sank like a stone before we could help them.

Many of these accidents were real accidents and could not have been avoided. I remember a friend of mine, Boy 1st Class Greenway, working a winch. We were getting in provisions port side forward. Just on the forecastle, his gloved hand caught in a snag of the wire which was going round the drum, and he was carried round with it and crushed before the shocked motor man could switch off and stamp his foot on the brake. This poor lad lived a few hours in agony, and then was glad to depart this world. But the iron discipline of war allowed us to ride these awful accidents and we were far too busy to stop to dwell on the consequences.

About that time the battle cruiser HMAS *Australia,* lent to the Fleet for the war by the Australian Government, joined us. This made another welcome addition to the Battle Cruiser Squadron. They were soon taking part in sport with us. I was now a member of the ship's water polo club and we challenged them to a game. A very nice signal came back, instigated by 'Boy' Charlton, the originator and inventor of that great swimming stroke, the 'Australian Crawl'. He was a world champion swimmer.

We played them very many times in the old South Queensferry baths and later in the war at the Carnegie Baths at Dunfermline. Of course, we never won a match but we gave them a good run for their money. Of course, it was Navy water polo – no holds barred, and really rough, but great fun. We were the only party at that time allowed ashore on leave; the men were all teetotal and trusted, being in the charge of Petty Officer Wheeler, who acted as referee.

Later, we played a league which included the ships of the

'Wobbly Eight', the pre-Dreadnoughts, battleships of the King Teddie Class, *Hibernia, Dominion, Commonwealth, Hindustan, Brittania, Africa, Zealandia* and, of course, the flagship, *King Edward VII*.

Just about this time, someone in authority had a brainwave, and what a brainwave it was! Observation balloons had been successfully used in the Western Front in France by the Army. Someone thought we could try them out in the Fleet but they had little idea of the difficulties entailed. The balloons were streamlined affairs, sausage-shaped, with a basket slung beneath for the observer's use. We had a good laugh about this because, of course, any seaman would know that it could not possibly work. All ships bolted a very sturdy electric winch on to the port after side of the after forecastle deck in preparation. Then all the battle cruisers steamed out to sea.

Very soon it became evident that the idea would not work and we were greatly amused. At any speed above six knots the wire hawsers and the balloon would not stand the strain; one balloon from one of the ships was carried away and was last seen disappearing with a trailing wire far over the distant horizon. I have no idea what happened eventually to the observer.

Our gallent adventurer was soon shouting down the telephone wire that we should winch him down, and that was at the speed of only four knots. All the balloons at that speed were dipping and prancing like fairground horses. At that moment I heard a remark passed: 'The bloke who thought up this idea was fitted for, but not with.' Our bloke was very glad to be down on *terra firma* on the upper deck.

Also about that time there appeared with the Fleet at sea the ridged and non-ridged type of airship. These were mostly of the streamlined, sausage-shaped type of dirigible and they had a small engine carried in a sort of framework cabin slung underneath. The engine power was not sufficient to enable them to keep up with the speed of the Fleet, so their use was rather limited. But I believe they were used for submarine patrol work later in the war.

The sea alarms and 'actions stations' were now all in a day's work and the loss of sleep we had to endure, but we became accustomed to the hardship of the routine after a time. However, sometimes when the weather was nice and warm that lovely summer, we could enjoy the music and beauty of the North Sea. A school of porpoises would dip and rise, peerless poetry of motion.

The summer sun glistened on their ebonite-like bodies, drops of water like falling diamonds scattering from their graceful forms as they made symmetrical arcs at our bows. The sea dappled by cloud wrack on a sunlit day made us feel that we, too, had our golden moments in the middle of the maelstrom of this dreadful war.

We learned about the progress of the war from the 'Poldhu Press', a Cornish wireless station which gave out censored news. Of course, this came over in Morse code. Our 'Sparkers' would receive it on the very efficient wireless sets, and type it out, to place it later on each notice board at nine o'clock in the morning. We used to sing out, 'Here come the morning papers' as we crowded round the news sheet to read mostly about the war on the Western Front.

This brings me to another event. We learned quite a lot about the Western Front in France from an exchange of senior NCOs and officers between Army and Navy. It was a splendid idea and taught both services just what their counterparts were doing to help win the war.

The Army NCOs would keep watch with us at the guns at sea and their officers would be up on the bridge, or in control positions. And in harbour they would talk to us about their life in the trenches. They also told the story of a petty officer from the Fleet who won a Distinguished Conduct Medal during a sudden trench raid. He had suddenly found himself surrounded by yelling Germans, but his unusual uniform saved him from being killed by the enemy troops. He seized a rifle from a dead Tommy and threw himself on them right and left, smiting them hip and thigh with bayonet and bullet. They fled in terror from the Blue Devil, and suddenly he realised that he was standing alone, breathing heavily, the steel in his hand dripping red, and the barrel of his rifle smoking hot.

Both arms of the Service declared that they would not permanently change places with one another. Every man to his trade – Brown Job or Blue Job.

Often we would race through the night at twenty-six knots to find at our dawn rendezvous perhaps off the North Hinder light vessel or off the Sylt Minefields, etc., an empty sea. There would be no enemy, just a desolate waste of tumbling waters. Jerry had scuttled back into harbour.

One night, that lovely early summer, during a periodical sweep into

German waters, we had drawn the usual blank and Beatty altered course north to meet Jellicoe's Battle Fleet coming south. We stood down from action stations and our gun crews had the 'dark afternoon', the middle watch. We were off the coast of Norway; about two o'clock I moved out on to the upper deck and with cupped hands was having a quiet smoke and a breath of fresh air. The sea was quiet and still like dark blue ice. Away out to the east the first flush of dawn was lighting up the curvature of the earth, and the lonely figure of 'Old Man Moon' hung low in the distant horizon. My thoughts were far away. I was thinking about my eldest brother fighting on the Western Front with the Gloucesters. My latest letter from my Mother had told me that he had been wounded, but no details.

Slowly I sensed that I was not alone and, turning, I saw that I had been joined by my chum, Sidney Cocking. He said in a low, awe-struck voice, 'What a lovely morning.'

I replied, 'Yes, daylight comes early here at this time of the year.'

The portals of the dawn were getting brighter every moment, and the eastward stars paled before the roseate flush. We gazed in wonder at the glorious scene. Suddenly the rim of the morning sun kissed the line of the horizon and burst into view. A ball of fire! It flamed the heavens over the placid sea, turning its colour from midnight blue to morning glory. It was like a page from a travel agent's dream world, poetic with its beauty. Later, just before we were relieved, we both came on deck again and the scene had changed. An off-shore breeze ruffled the calm sea like rippled silk. Slowly we both became aware of the scent in the air, and Sidney said, 'Can you smell what I smell?'

I said, 'Yes – country wild flowers, like a walk down an English lane.' As I spoke, a flock of migrant birds darkened the sky and then were gone. As we turned to go below decks to our hammocks we took one last look at the scene. The lazy pacing clouds of various hues patched, like paved mosaics, the vault of heaven, and away out on the far horizon a few shark-finned sails dotted the skyline.

I remember the German Grand Admiral Tirpitz had said, 'I'll have them always at sea, and I'll wear them down.'

We refused to be worn down. We defeated his object by dividing the whole Fleet into three watches on each ship – red, white and blue. During the watches we manned one 13.5 inch turret and two 6 inch guns, and the magazines for these weapons, also control positions, etc. One watch kept the first watch 8-12 p.m., then the morning watch from 4-8 a.m.; and then one watch kept the afternoon 12.30-4 p.m. with the middle watch 12-4 a.m. at night. The watch that kept the first and morning had the last dog 6-8 p.m. and then all night in their hammocks. The middle watch kept the forenoon watch 8 a.m.-12.30 p.m. and then the first dog 4-6 p.m. By this means, men were able to combat the long hours at sea closed up ready for action and, of course, the very hard work of coaling ship in harbour. But, of course, in German waters we would all be awake, closed up ready for action, perhaps for as long as thirty-six hours at a time. In harbour and at sea the care and maintenance of the ship was done in the forenoon, and if possible we slept during the afternoon, so you can see that if we were not too busy we were able to rest.

Often we would have a file of Marines up on deck firing rifles at drifting mines to render them safe by exploding them. The spring-loaded safety pistol which under the Hague Convention should render all moored mines that broke away from their anchorage safe, did not always work, and a 'drifter' was always regarded as dangerous. Sometimes the wicked-looking 'horns' would be hit and with a loud bang a great gout of flame would follow, and sometimes the mine casing would be pierced by a bullet and the buoyancy chamber filled with sea water. The missile would then sink to the ocean floor out of harm's way.

The submarine warfare on our maritime trade was now becoming serious, and about this time a messmate of mine, Able Seaman Isaac Foot, a Brixham trawlerman, was asked to volunteer for the first 'Q' Boat (the submarine decoy ships).

Later in the war he returned to us all smiles. A couple of ships had been sunk under him, but having earned the DCM he was quite pleased and rightly proud of the medal ribbon sewn to his left breast. Later he was decorated by the King.

We were ably led by a splendid officer team, Captain Pelly being particularly fortunate in this respect. 'Togo' Davies was a very fine upper-deck commander who had a flair for managing the ship's company in difficult circumstances. Our gunnery officer, Commander Macnamara, was a very efficient type and every morning at sea or in harbour we would be doing some type of gunnery practice: sub-calibre, or one inch rifle firing, or at the laying and training teacher. All these drills would simulate the real thing in one form or another. In harbour or at sea we were always firing at targets. Often the whole Squadron would proceed to sea and fire at a towed battle practice target. Yes, we were becoming very efficient. These drills, of course, would include everyone else in the fighting efficiency of the ship; everyone was taught and kept at the highest peak of his particular job in action.

A lovely summer faded, the air was chilled with the rumour of winter, and soon across the North Sea the mists returned in great swirling banks, and we had to be even more alert. We were told that the Germans had a new Commander-in-Chief, a man with a more aggressive spirit, and everyone knew that one day there would be a show-down.

The U-boat menace was always with us and our look-outs had a tremendous responsibility. Of course, the loneliest job was that of the signal man up in the crow's nest. It was also the coldest job. On a clear day the look-out could see the smoke of a ship well beyond fifteen miles right around the horizon. A puff of smoke seen through his high-powered binoculars would find him pressing the alarm buzzer to the officer of the watch far below him on the upper bridge on 'Monkey's Island'. This look-out, of course, was a very efficient protection. He could also well spot the tell-tale wake of an enemy torpedo but it was in foggy or misty weather that we had to be particularly alert. Later in the war, while on patrol, we would steer a zig-zag course to make it hard for a U-boat to line up her periscope sights.

Our light forces were a very fine collection of ships led by Commodores Goodenough and Sir Alexander Sinclair, flying their broad pennants in *Southampton* and *Galatea*. These ships were modern and fast with 6 inch guns and torpedo tubes firing a good output.

Winter came all too soon but this time we were well equipped to meet the rigours of the weather. We were well supplied with rubber sea boots, duffle suits, trousers and coats, white woollen thigh-length oiled stockings, and leather fleecy-lined mittens secured to the necks of our duffle coats by means of a rope cord.

In harbour, the boat crews suffered from frostbite; many of the seamen drowned, being swept overboard by the rough weather, and their sea boots filling with water they sank like a stone before they could be rescued. Sir David gave orders that the men were to wear rubber gym shoes and to be tied by a life-line to the funnel casings. That order stopped the loss of life.

It was about this time that I witnessed another dramatic incident in sea warfare. We were out at sea with the Grand Fleet in cruising formation with *Dreadnought* stationed just off our starboard bow. I was off watch and was just looking around when the incident happened. I saw most of it, but the gaps in my knowledge were filled in later.

A shout of 'Periscope ahead, sir,' from a look-out with a given bearing, a blast on the siren, which made me look towards the '*Donut*'. The siren alarm called the Fleet's attention to alter course. The Captain gave a 'cracking helm order' and the great steel ram of her bows arrowed straight into the guts of a U-boat – wham! There was a sickening crunch and the scream of outraged metal, and she appeared to climb the '*Donut*'s' stem, hanging there like a huge wounded whale; then silently she slipped back and disappeared, the weight of the great ship driving her down, a steel coffin, to the ocean floor a hundred fathoms deep.

A few hurried signals and we learned that we had avenged the loss of the three old armoured cruisers sunk by this submarine in 1914 – the *Hogue, Aboukir* and *Cressy*. That was the end of the *U-29,* Otto Weddingen and his renowned crew. Swiftly, and without warning, they had found out what it was like to be on the receiving end. The fortunes of war, indeed. We felt that there was never a dull moment in our routine.

That winter we found ourselves once more on Arctic Patrol. We bagged the job because our Admiral said that the *Tiger* would want no escort; with her great speed she could look after herself. Off the Lofoten Islands we ran into a great storm. It was night time, and by four bells in the middle watch, being unable to sleep due to the ship's pitching, I found myself on the hard deck, shot out of my hammock, and looking around in the blue phosphorescent light of the dimmed lamps and sloshing sea, found my drifting sea boots, full of salt water. I dressed and went up on deck. Standing underneath the signal bridge, I watched the lightning running up and down the vane and truck, and dancing along the triatic stay. And amidst the howling of a banshee wind, the roll and crack of thunder, the ship shook like a toy in the hands of a giant.

I surveyed the scene and listened. It was as if a colossal orchestra was playing with mighty volume the storm music from Wagner's *Flying Dutchman*. And, when dawn broke, the steelwork of our superstructures glistened like silver with packed ice. On the forecastle screen in places the paint had been worn off, showing the red lead beneath. Great scarlet weals had been licked off by the angry, smoking seas. The wind still sounded like some fierce tuneless opera directed by a mad conductor – an orchestra from the orbs of hell.

Soon we got to work to free our guns and so on with hot water hoses and chipping hammers. It took some time to get battleworthy. We soon returned after this to our Squadron as Sir David Beatty wanted us back.

The Battle Cruiser Squadron was now complete. All the ships that were doing duty in the Outer Seas had returned, and were with us at Rosyth. So Jellicoe dispensed with the pre-Dreadnoughts, the 'Wobbly Eight'. The *King Edward VII* was lost off the Irish coast, striking a mine, and the remainder departed to the Mediterranean. While on passage they nearly lost the *Albemarle*; a great storm rendered her out of control going through the dreaded Pentland Skerries, and for a while she became a drifting hulk. Next morning, a couple of ocean-going tugs from Scapa managed to get hold of her and towed her to the lee of the land. This occurred in the dreaded stretch of water leading from the North Sea out to the broad sweep of the Atlantic.

The Battle Cruiser Fleet now comprised three complete Squadrons: the 1st, *Lion,* Fleet flagship, Admiral Sir David Beatty; *Princess Royal,* Rear-Admiral O. de B. Brock; *Queen Mary,* and our ship, *Tiger*. The 2nd Squadron: *New Zealand*, flag of Rear-Admiral Pakenham, *Indefatigable*, and *Australia.* The 3rd Squardon: *Invincible,* flying the flag of the Rear-Admiral, the Hon. Horace Hood, *Inflexible* and *Indomitable*.

A fine, hard hitting fleet of battle cruisers, the speed of the whole fleet being 28 knots, with powerful modern 13.5 inch and 12 inch guns mounted in four twin turrets. Little wonder Beatty was proud of his mighty fleet. And with our attendant light forces, cruisers and destroyers, we were a magnificent striking force. We really were battleworthy now and there was a feeling afoot that *Der Tag*, the German words for 'The Day', was not far off. A trial of strength must come.

We knew that Hipper had a new battle cruiser for his flagship, the *Lützow*, a new ship worked up and ready for action, a really hard hitting ship. We could sense that the time was not far off and we dreamed about it and prayed for victory. There is no doubt about it: the whole Grand Fleet was in a similar mood. Jellicoe's vast array of mighty ships was trained to the very limit and just raring to go, from the Commander-in-Chief down to the humblest midshipman and boy.

I must return awhile and tell you what a wonderful Christmas we had in 1915; actually we were in harbour and it was the best Christmas of the war. There was plenty of good food, turkeys, plum duff, mincement pies, etc. for everyone to enjoy. We had lots of parcels from home and other well-wishers, and many a bottle of Scotch and Irish whisky found its way from the wardroom to the troops' messes. Lady Beatty, who was the daughter of an American millionaire, provided us with a little extra from her personal yacht *Sheelah* lying anchored close to the *Lion*'s buoy. She was always very good and did a lot to look after the welfare of her husband's 'boys'. Our good friend, Lord Elgin, gave us garlands for the masts and yards. It was a real Christmas with the holly and the ivy.

We had a famous character, our forecastle officer, who was a regular Jack Harkaway straight from the pages of Marryat's *Midshipman Easy*. A more dare-devil officer one never met. I can see him now, leading the gay sparks from the wardroom down through our ill-lit mess decks, his naked form draped with a Union Jack, drunk as a lord, helping to carry 'Togo' Davies, our good Commander, shoulder-high and cheering like mad. The Marine Band, sadly out of tune, trailed behind playing 'Life on the Ocean Wave'.

What a day! We all saved up our rum ration (strictly illegal, of course) and, with the officers' wines and spirits, we got into the true Christmas festive mood. It was a time to remember, the order of the day being 'Today we live, tomorrow we may die'.

That evening, we finished up with an impromptu concert on the quarterdeck, men's mess decks, one each side of the ship. In fact, there were two concerts running at the same time, the artists performing twice. The day closed with the 'Sky Pilot' leading us with that great carol 'Silent Night'. The first two verses were sung by a very young boy 2nd Class, who had arrived that morning in a draft from HMS *Impregnable,* the harbour training ship. Our Chaplain informed us that he was an ex-chorister from a well-beloved West Country cathedral. He stole our hearts away with his sweet young voice, standing before us, hands clasped, a diminutive figure with a face like a herald angel, six weeks in the Navy, about to be flung into battle. 'Holy Night! Silent Night!' His sweet soprano voice soared and echoed through the fan shafts; we deep water men were held enthralled, spellbound with the magic of that nightingale wearing three rows of tapes, and then, with the padre beating time, we joined in with the last verse! The greatest carol service I have ever heard.

As the closing notes died away, a deep hush fell on the congregation, then someone started to clap the little lad. Soon a storm of applause swept through the mess deck like a tidal wave. Then, bowing, the padre and the choir-boy left the starboard quarterdeck men's mess deck to repeat this performance on the port side, following by a scrambling crowd of sailormen.

Our good chaplain later returned to say a goodnight prayer.

Next morning, very bleary-eyed, we got the greenery down from the masts and yards, luckily without accident. Then the capstan and cable holders rattling merrily, the anchors were soon aweigh and we were waving to our soldier friends guarding the Forth Bridge. We steamed out to sea past May Island for the umpteenth time.

By this time I had joined with the electrical party and I was being trained for a torpedo man. This, of course, did not alter my action station. It was a Fleet order that no officer or man should change his action station in spite of promotion. So, of course, I remained a loading number at S.3 gun. We were so well trained in gunnery that if required we could have entered a turret and helped to fight the great 13.5 inch heavies.

And so the New Year was born and we went on our way, secure in the knowledge that we really knew our job and were fighting fit. Spring came early that year in the North Sea and the mists melted away from the grey waters.

Up at Scapa we met the Russian cruiser *Askold*, the first of the Allied warships to join the Fleet, having done good work out in the Mediterranean. She was known to our Fleet men as 'The Packet of Woodbines' on account of her five thin long close-together funnels. Woodbine cigarettes were sold five in a little green packet for one penny in those days of cheap living.

In harbour I often went on board the *New Zealand*. A Cheltenham friend of mine, a 'Towny', served on board this fine ship which was a gift from the New Zealand Government. We would often stand beneath the ship's crest with the magic word 'Ao-tea-roa' – the 'Great White Cloud'. The ship had been painted white when serving in Dominion waters.

The greatest of all the Maori chiefs said, when blessing the ship, that nothing serious would go wrong with her, providing the Captain wore the sacred garments which he provided for that purpose in action. These good luck charms did save the ship. She went right through the war with hardly any damage and very little loss of life. The same thing happened to the *Ajax*, which fought so well in the Second World War.

My friend and I were talking quietly on the *New Zealand* upper deck while in harbour one Sunday, and discussing our chances of getting to grips with the enemy. He told me that Sir David Beatty had remarked that Jerry would not build such a large fleet just to allow it to rust away in harbour. 'No,' I replied, 'they will try and catch a detached Squadron and wipe it out, and so whittle away the strength of the Grand Fleet.' How right our train of thought was.

The nights grew shorter and the days longer and it soon became a pleasure once more to be at sea. We know the routine well and could more or less guess where we were without asking the bridge messenger to have a look at the charts. The throb of the questing lead would tell us that we were off the Dogger Bank. One could hear the whine of the electric motor anywhere on the upper deck.

Eastward in German waters the sea would be a greyish-green at most times of the year. This would occur in patches and if the sky was light it would turn to a peculiar shade of blue.

That April we had several false alarms and in early May Jerry did come out. It was to be another raid on the east coast of England, but the German Battle Cruiser Squadron did not get very far. The *Moltke* politely exploded one of our mines and had several armoured plates stove in. The whole Squadron returned to harbour. We had known they were coming out because we had all the secrets of the German wireless codes. These were obtained when the German cruiser *Magdeburg* was mined in Russian waters and a diver went down, to find a dead signal officer with the secret code books clasped in his arms. All this had occurred early in the war and the secret books were rushed to England by a fast cruiser. In addition, our directional wireless finding stations had now reached a high state of efficiency.

Admiralty Intelligence was also very well served with probable enemy movements and other vital information, and this was promptly passed on.

Getting back to this planned raid on our east coast, we were steaming hard to meet them but we, too, ran into trouble. During a violent alter course at night, the *New Zealand* and *Australia* collided. Luckily, only the latter was damaged enough to order docking. The *New Zealand* more or less got away without serious injury – the lucky ship once again!

The Admiralty were now fairly confident that Jerry was planning something bigger than a raid. Everything pointed to a large-scale sortie very soon. Quietly, we prepared.

CHAPTER 7

# Jutland

*'The Greatest Naval Action the World has ever known.'* Admiral of the Fleet, Lord Fisher of Kilverstone.

## *The Opening Shots*

On the evening of 30th May 1916, we left Rosyth. The whole of the Battle Cruiser Force sailed as one unit. This included the 1st, 2nd and 3rd Light Cruiser Squadron and the 9th, 10th and 13th Destroyer Flotillas.

The 3rd Battle Cruiser Squadron, the *Invincible, Inflexible* and *Indomitable*, were exercising up at Scapa Flow and their places had been taken by the 5th Battle Squadron, the Queen Elizabeth Class of fast modern battleships, probably the most powerful ships in the world. The flagship *Barham* flying the flag of Vice-Admiral Evan Thomas, with the *Valiant, Malaya* and *Warspite,* the *Queen Elizabeth* being in dry dock.

These magnificent warships sailed with us under the overall flag of Sir David Beatty's command. This, of course, was because of their great speed of 25 knots, or a little more if pushed. This was faster than any other type of battleship. Almost at the same time Jellicoe left Scapa with his great fleet of sixteen Dreadnought battleships, plus heavy and light cruiser squadrons, and five flotillas of destroyers. They steamed at 16 knots to rendezvous east of the 'Long Forties', there to meet the 2nd Battle Squadron out from Cromarty – eight more battleships.

By a strange oversight, the *Campania*, the most modern seaplane carrier in the world, was left in some far-off corner of 'Flotta', due to not receiving the signal to sail in time to proceed with the Fleet. This was to prove later a great disadvantage. The *Engadine*, the other seaplane carrier, sailed with us from Rosyth. These carriers were designed only for float planes but pioneers like Flight-Lieutenant Rutland were experimenting and had actually flown off their decks with a tiny monoplane.

| Distance run through the Water | Course and Distance made good | Latitude (N) |
|---|---|---|
| 463' | As Reqt. | D.R. 56° 20<br>Obs. |

| Variation | True Bearing and Distance | Currents in the 2… |
|---|---|---|
| 14° – 12° W | Honis Reef L.V.<br>S.SE. 57' | |

| | | | | | | | | | |
|---|---|---|---|---|---|---|---|---|---|
| 1 | 18 | 0 | As Reqt. | | Var. | | | | |
| | 9 | 0 | – | | – | | | | |
| 2 | 9 | 0 | N 16° W | nil | 170·1 | | | | |
| 3 | 18 | 0 | – | – | 171·8 | | | | |
| 4 | 18 | 0 | – | – | Var. | S.W.by S. | 4 | bc. | 3 |
| 5 | 18 | 0 | – | – | – | | | | |
| | 8 | 0 | – | – | – | | | | |
| 6 | 10 | 0 | S 89° W | – | – | South | 4 | o.c | 3 |
| 7 | 18 | 0 | – | – | – | | | | |
| 8 | 19 | 0 | – | – | 196·4 | South | 4 | oc. | 3 |
| 9 | 21 | 0 | – | – | 200·2 | | | | |
| 10 | 21. | 0 | – | – | 198·4 | | | | |
| 11 | 21 | 0 | – | – | 198·8 | | | | |
| 12 | 21 | 0 | – | – | 198·4 | South | 4 | oc. | 3 |

Extract from *Tiger*'s Log for 31st May 1916. *Reproduced by courtesy of the Public Records Office.*

| Longitude (E) | Number on Sick List |
|---|---|
| 6° 20' | 43 |

ours ending at Noon

/

**Provisions received**

| | lbs. |
|---|---|
| Fresh Meat | |
| Vegetables | |
| Bread | |

**Fresh Water**

| | Tons |
|---|---|
| Received | 0 |
| Distilled | |
| Expended | 20 |
| Remaining | 150 |

**Fuel**

| Expended for all purposes | Tons |
|---|---|
| Coal | 377 |
| Oil | 157 |
| **Remaining** | **Tons** |
| Coal | 2286 |
| Oil | 484 |

P.M.

1·30 a/c N 16° W

| | | | |
|---|---|---|---|
| 29·50 | 50 | 50 | IV ——— 0 ——— 0 ——— |

5·25 a/c S 89° W

| | | | |
|---|---|---|---|
| 29·48 | 48 | 47 | VI-0 Formed single quarter line to port and committed bodies of Mr [illegible] (Chief Bos'n) & Mr. [illegible] ([illegible]) & 24 ratings killed in action to the deep. |
| | | | 6·28 [illegible] |
| | | | 7·0 Formed single line ahead. Hauled out of line to fire lyddite common from B turret & six 6" guns. |
| | | | 7·30 Speed 21 knots |
| 29·45 | 46 | 45 | VIII ——— 0 ——— 0 ——— |
| | | | Resumed place in line |
| 29·30 | 44 | 44 | XII ——— 0 ——— 0 ——— |

The weather was fine but the night was dark, and as expected Jerry had a submarine net flung out across all entrances to the Fleet anchorages. But all enemy torpedoes missed their mark and I strongly suspect that both Jellicoe and Beatty altered course from their usual route at the critical moment. These, then, were the enemy's opening shots, had we only known it at the time. It was all a part of the great plan of attrition but it did not succeed. Several 'tin fish' were spotted or, rather, their phosphorescent wakes, and that was that. We steamed safely away from the danger zone. Von Scheer's plan had come adrift.

That evening, I came off the last dog watch at 8 p.m. and went down to supper. The last dog watch, of course, gave the welcome all night in one's hammock. Immediately before turning in I went for a walk round.

Up on deck the night was calm, quiet, dark and with no stars. The air was clean and fresh and I walked back again through the double black canvas screened after forecastle doors. I look a turn around the covered-in battery deck; to me it seemed strangely quiet.

The decks were deserted and lit dimly by blue electric lights, which emitted a ghostly glow. I am sure any prowling U-boat would not have observed us as we slipped quietly through the dark waters. There was hardly anyone about. I saw only one solitary stoker gazing at the one and only crown and anchor board situated on the top of an upturned rum tub.

The whole air of the usual busy recreation space was one of desolation. I gazed at the gilt letters of 'God Save The King' in reverse on the rum tub. Then I realised that for some reason the ship's company was interested only in getting into their hammocks and going to sleep. We all sensed that something was coming, but did not know what.

I, too, wondered what it might be, but refused to guess.

### *The Battle of Jutland, 31st May 1916*

The first part of this action is termed by naval historians as 'The Run to the South' and it was the clash between the opposing battle cruisers. All night long we headed for our rendezvous off the coast of Jutland at the reduced speed of 18 knots. The coastline was the northern fringe of the Heligoland Bight, German waters.

In 'line ahead' our outposts, the 1st Light Cruiser Squadron flagship, *Galatea,* flying the broad pennant of Commodore Alexander Sinclair; in the centre was the *Falmouth*, flagship of the 3rd Light Cruiser Squadron, and the 2nd LCS *Southampton* and her consorts on the starboard wing.

This was the position at 2 p.m. on 31st May 1916.

Having reached the agreed position, Beatty hoisted the turning signal and with the answering pennant 'At the dip', the whole Fleet, apart from the light cruisers, turned north. He was about to take his great fleet to rendezvous with Jellicoe fifty miles ahead of his position.

Commodore Sinclair and his light cruisers did not answer the 'alter course' signal but hung on for a while, owing to the presence of a merchant ship. The vessel appeared to be 'blowing off steam' and the Commodore was curious.

A moment later came a shout from the masthead man up aloft in the crow's nest. By means of a megaphone, he called everyone's attention on the flagship bridge to the fact that the unmistakable stump mast of a German destroyer was visible. She, too, was curious, and was asking the merchantman if she had seen anything of the British Fleet.

Immediately action stations was sounded and soon the first shots of the Jutland Battle were being fired. The noise of battle rolled across the peaceful waters of the Skagerrak with startling suddenness.

The *Galatea* and her consorts of all light cruiser squadrons increased speed to about 28 knots, and the first sighting enemy reports were going out by wireless. Suddenly things began to move. Up over the horizon came the enemy's screen of light forces. These were the German Rostock Class of light cruiser, plus the destroyer escorts.

The weather was very clear and soon the range closed to about 14,000 yards, the extreme range of the British light cruisers' 6 inch gun. A running fight ensued. Commodore Sinclair realised that his duty was to fall back on to our main force and keep reporting the situation, so, after the exchange of a few shots with the opposing light forces, he swung the whole of the 1st, 2nd and 3rd Light Cruiser Squadron around in a northerly direction. The 'enemy in sight' signal was picked up in both Fleet flagships, *Iron Duke,* Sir John Jellicoe with the battle fleet, and *Lion*, Sir David Beatty with the battle cruisers.

I had the afternoon watch at S.I. 6 inch emergency gun crew and all was quiet when I finished my 'trick' (duty) on the voice pipe at one-thirty p.m. Then, dozing in the corner of the gun casement, I gradually became aware of the fact that the ship was increasing speed.

For a while I did nothing because it really was not unusual, then suddenly I heard a ship's siren. Now this, I knew, was a warning signal, such as submarine alarm. The warning hoot was heard again so I looked at the battered German alarm clock hanging on a steel hook. The time was just after three o'clock. I must have been asleep!

I walked out on to the upper deck and a hurrying messenger brushed past me, exclaiming that the *Engadine* had just flown off a Short seaplane (this carrier would, of course, have hoisted out the seaplane on to the water by means of a derrick). And as he climbed the ladder leading up to the lower bridge he called out, 'I think there is something doing.'

I thought the same thing because, looking across at the battle cruisers, I noticed we were all battling along, flat out, great bow waves cresting away from our forefronts, and numerous hoists of flags from the signal deck yard arms.

From deck level little else could be seen so I climbed to the top steps of the steel starboard boom ladder, where I saw the destroyers going hell for leather, and a great heavy pall of smoke away to the south-east. For a moment I stood gazing at the sight, while I knew that something was certainly doing, and my senses quickened.

Suddenly the raucous notes of a bosun mate piping the red watch to 'down guard rails' sent me hurrying back into my gun casement. Our voice pipe number told me that something was doing and I told him all I knew. We promptly wakened the remainder of the gun crew.

Soon came the expected bugle call of action stations, its clarion notes stirring everyone to feverish activity. We were soon alerted to the fact that the German battle cruisers were out. We leapt to our feet and waited anxiously to be relieved by the proper gun crew so that we could man our own gun S. 3.

Out ahead of the great battle cruiser force the scouts of our fleet were reporting the presence of the German battle cruisers, their course and speed. On receipt of the 'enemy in sight' signal just after 2.15 p.m., Beatty had once again reversed his course to south. When

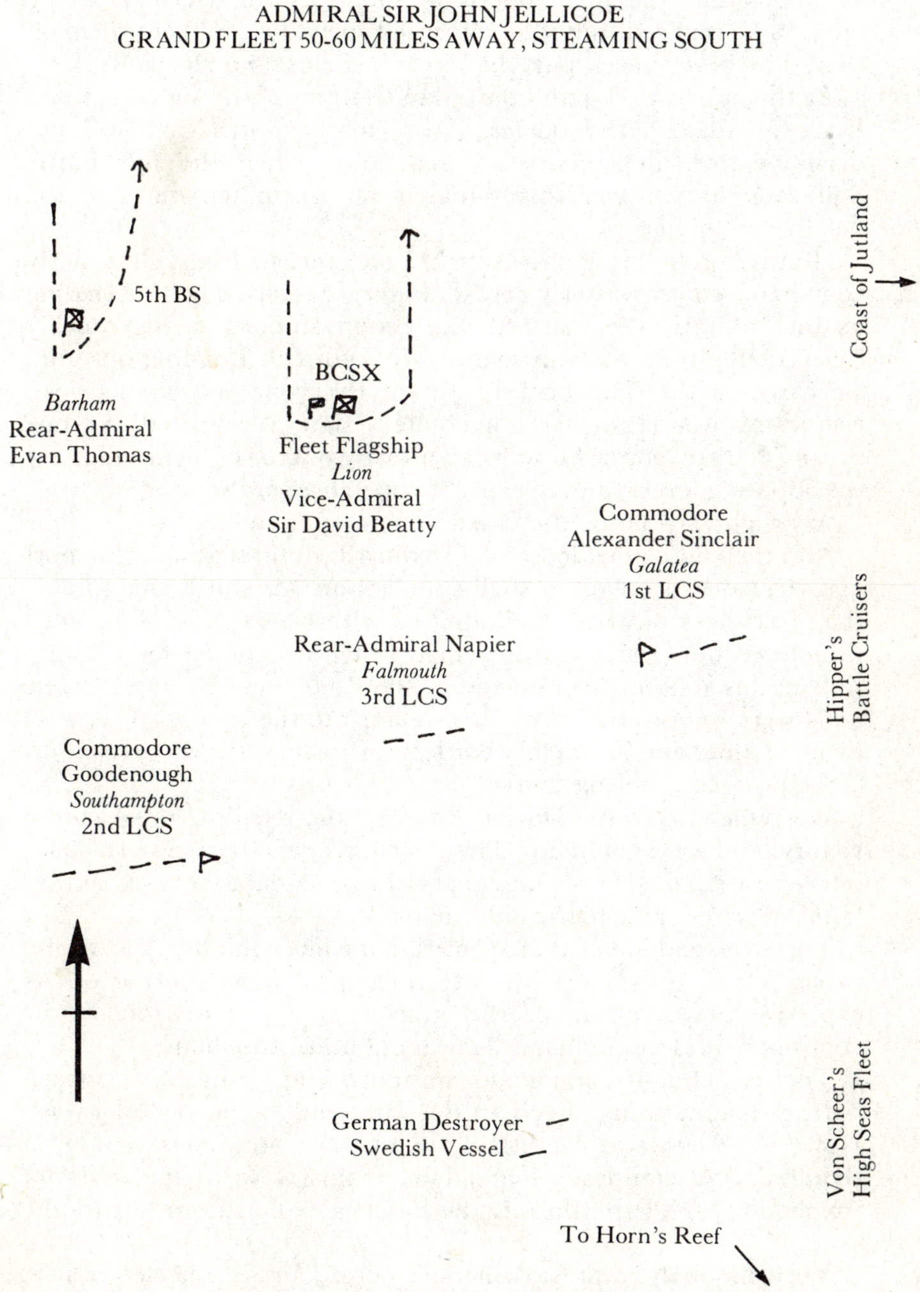


Situation at about 2.10 p.m. Rough Plan

he knew that the force opposing him was the German battle cruisers he realised that if he increased speed he could cut them off from their home bases, past the Vyl Minefields, and Horns Reef.

At this juncture, by an unavoidable failure of the signal system, Evan Thomas in the *Barham,* away to the north east, did not decipher the 'alter course' signal; thus when the 5th Battle Squadron did answer this signal it put them ten miles to the northwards of *Lion*.

Hipper, on sighting the British force, turned from a northerly course to a south-westerly course. Later we realised he was leading us into a trap. We manned our action stations, being quickly relieved; the time was approximately 3.40 p.m. Loading our gun, we came to the 'half cock' position. Everyone was at his post, everything was ready for immediate action. We waited. No one spoke. The gun control tower had already told us of the positions of the opposing forces, and to expect to open fire very soon.

At roughly 3.48 p.m. the *Lion* fired a ranging shot.

And then all hell let loose! A blinding flash through our gun port and the rattle of a hail of shell splinters on our ship's side told us that Jerry was already straddling us with a near miss. Our guns thundered out, the great 13.5 inch heavies speaking for the first time in this action. The range was some 18,000 yards distance. The odds were in our favour, six British ships to the enemy's five, with Evan Thomas and his mighty battleships cutting corners to make up for being late in altering course.

We remembered the Dogger Bank action, recalling the eventual victory, and were confident. That, of course, had been a stern chase but here we had the advantage of being on similar courses so that both sides were able to fire full broadsides.

The Armageddon of War seemed to me like a mighty Ajax trying to crack the Universe with a terrible, prolonged roaring of the explosive power of the fearful guns. The noise was absolutely continuous and we could hardly hear one another's shouts.

The tremendous cannonade continued and we in the starboard battery had nothing much to do, our guns being out of range. However, we made everything ready for continuous action, if required. We could see that all our ships were in the midst of tremendous shell splashes as the missiles exploded on hitting the seas.

Very suddenly, amidst deafening noise, our ship heeled over to the hammer of a tremendous shock and my mind rolled and spun like quicksilver. Then she seemed to shake herself like a dog with a bloody nose and then belted on at the speed of the Fleet, her guns hammering forth in a blazing torrent of ranging defiance. We had taken a full salvo right forward, beyond the great wheel-operated armoured door, and everything forrard was wiped out.

However, all was well. We were very much in action again. The range remained roughly about 18,000 wards, and time and again we felt the impact of exploding shells. No doubt about it, we were in the thick of it.

Suddenly, a few minutes later, the ship seemed to lift bodily sidewards and we received the worst hit we had had until then. Just one shell only had exploded underneath the warrant officers' mess, through the ship-side armoured belt, and into a storeroom below. A great fire raged around the ammunition passages and the port after 6 inch magazine had to be flooded to save the ship from blowing up.

The German 12 inch shell did an immense amount of damage and almost brought the ship to a standstill.

A shell fragment penetrated the port engine room and shattered a bracket holding the main steam pipe. The whole of that part of the engine room was filled with black acrid smoke which eventually cleared. The great pipe sagged but held and did not fracture, so the ship righted herself and, still roaring out with her great guns, still defiant, now became deadly with her execution, her shells bursting all over what appeared to our communications number to be the third ship of the enemy line. Our *Tiger* cleaved on through the shell-torn water at the great speed of 28 knots.

Our gunlayer and trainer, being outside the ship, passed a lot of information to us and occasionally we went into their seats to have a look for ourselves. Our friend up in the gun control tower kept up a running commentary on the situation as he saw it, and any information he gleaned from the motley collection of voice pipes all round him.

The spotting top voice pipes were close to his head and he received quite a lot of information regarding what the gunnery officer could see, and what the various ships were doing. This included information from the 13.5 inch main director tower and quite a bit of what was said by the Captain and his staff. These voice pipes were linked together in a small compartment known as the 'Voice Pipe Exchange'. Of course, the information he learned was somewhat garbled but, being an astute lad, he sorted most of it out, and some of the news we got was of a positive nature.

His remarks about the enemy's fall of shot not being spread as it should have been was surprising, because at the Dogger Bank action the wide spread was one thing we all noticed. The enemy's fire control arrangements must have been altered. We all knew they did not have director fire the same as we had, where all guns fired together either an eight or four gun salvo, that is, both guns in each turret, or just one; when all sights came on from the director tower, all gunlayers and trainers kept the guns pointing on to the targets by means of the director electrical instruments.

Our friend in the gun control tower also observed that our ships were continually altering course slightly to throw off the enemy's fire.

Suddenly, just after 4 p.m. he said in a dull voice, 'Sorry, chums, but we've lost the *Indefatigable.*' He was right. The *Indefatigable* had blown up, her forward magazine exploding in a great plume of smoke and fire. All hands were lost but two, 1017 officers and men.

Then we scored our first major success. The look-out in the crow's nest reported while looking through his powerful binoculars that one of the German ships had reeled out of line, blazing fore and aft. Actually this was not quite correct, but the *Seydlitz* had her Dogger Bank experience repeated all over again. Her two after turrets had blown up with a tremendous roaring spurt of flame which reached well over the height of her foremast. Nearly 200 officers and men perished in that blazing inferno, including the ammunition passage crews who were incinerated by a wall of fire. Well shot, the *Queen Mary*! Our wonderful crack gunnery ship had really got going now, and also the *Lion.* If anything, these two ships seemed to have more success than the remainder of the Fleet, but from all the information we received there was no doubt that our battle cruisers were doing very well.

The first few minutes of the action we failed to get the range, due to smoke. We knew the German rangefinders were far more accurate than ours.

Then we received another bad hit and so did the *Lion,* due to the enemy's point of aim being the foremast and the drift aft mostly made the shots hit amidships. Our 'Q' turret was badly hit, a heavy shell penetrating the centre sighting hood of the rooftop and killing one officer and three men, besides wounding one officer and many men. Due, however, to the magnificent efforts of the turret officer, and Petty Officer Fitzgerald, they managed to get the turret back into action.

Some of the spare crew were brought up from below and with hand loading, the gun loading cage being jammed in the Down position, the left gun spoke again.

In *Lion*, the same thing had happened but with more serious results, the whole turret being gutted with flames from ignited cordite charges. The Captain of Marines in his last dying moments ordered his already wounded Sergeant up on to the bridge to report to the Captain of the ship that he had ordered the magazine to be flooded, and thus saved the ship from blowing up.

Many men died in this fearful disaster because the fire travelled down the turret trunk and killed everyone below. The switchboard crew and electrical repair parties perished in the blazing inferno adjacent to the passages close to the magazine.

We watched the *Lion* many hours during the action, and smoke continued to pour from her 'Q' turret roof. However, fortunately she was able to continue the action with her other six 13.5 inch guns. Later the Captain of Marines was posthumously awarded a well-deserved Victoria Cross.

Returning to our own ship, suddenly we were told by our gun control tower friend that 'X' turret had not come to the 'Ready'. The 'Gun Ready' lamps did not burn, indicating that the turret was out of action. This hit was not serious and the after turret soon came back with a mighty roar of flame. The turret, our Marine turret, had had a shell explode outside the great steel barbette. Unfortunately, the concussion from the explosion killed our second postman and the dynamo firing circuits were cut. The turret electrician soon repaired the wires. Just after this I was invited by our gunlayer to change places with him, and on climbing into his seat I got a ringside view of the contest.

A delightful surprise met my gaze – a silent ship with a pyramid of white canvas met my eyes, serene, quiet and peaceful. Her three masts towered to the heavens, a large barque lying almost becalmed, just moving gently through the water with all her sails set, rippling with the light breeze, her canvas only half filled. She moved gracefully like a great swan. Then I remembered we had had the same moving experience in the Dogger Bank action. Such a beautiful sight amidst the horror and fearful hate of the shell-torn waters was almost unbelievable.

Both sides were firing well, but now we were definitely on top. Jerry's salvos were nowhere near as accurate as in the early minutes of the action. A remark from the gun control tower told us that Evan Thomas was now coming into action with his splendid squadron of 15 inch gunned battleships.

At the extreme range of 22,000 yards, the 5th Battle Squadron Admiral had, by cutting corners, been able to bring his ships into action. His leading ships were firing at the rear of Hipper's squadron and the *Moltke* and *Von Der Tann* began to feel the terrible effect of the exploding armour-piercing shells. Great plumes of water spouted from the enemy's position as gunfire engulfed the ships. Beatty now had the situation well in hand and at irregular intervals all ships were slightly altering course, to dodge the fall of enemy shot.

Then the smoke from our destroyers, which had gradually drawn ahead, began to foul the range and Beatty made a definite 'alter course' to get clear. This 'alter course' was further away from the enemy – away to starboard from the main southerly course, and the range opened out.

The two lines of fast-moving ships sped on southwards, great orange flashes coming from their guns, and occasionally a dull mushroom flame blossomed forth from the upper works of ships, meaning the detonating devastation of another hit as the shells exploded.

Both sides were now equal; that is, of course, not entirely correct – the 5th Battle Squadron was slowly coming within range and exceeding their designed speed – but with the *Indefatigible* gone it was five ships – that is, battle cruisers, to five of the enemy's. But now, with the advent of the 5th Battle Squadron, Jerry's fire had slackened a little, which was of course understandable.

The thing which impressed us most was that their shells were missing by a considerable distance, and our friend on top was in a happy mood, crying out the old-time gunnery phrase, 'All hits in the blue count!' meaning, of course, all hits in the sea.

This error in their gunnery was put down to the fact that their rangefinders were of a more delicate nature, and were being put out by the concussion of the gunfire from their own guns. Also the explosion of our shells was damaging the delicate mechanism by their concussive effects. Many years later, I learned that Jerry had at the beginning of the action fired the whole battery of his secondary armament guns, which in some cases were approximately 5 inch calibre, into the sea, just outside their own ships, to indicate to our spotting officers our fall of shot. Our well-trained gunnery spotters soon observed that trick and took no notice of the artful move.

Curious thing, our gunnery officer, Commander Macnamara, told us later during a lecture that he found that medium-powered glasses were more effective than the high magnification binoculars, and after the first quarter of an hour he used medium Barr & Stroud glasses.

The *Lion* was now firing at her opposite number, the *Lützow, Princess Royal* firing at *Derfflinger, Queen Mary* at *Seydlitz, Tiger* at *Moltke*, and *New Zealand* firing briskly away at *Von Der Tann*. Our *New Zealand*, the last ship in our line, was doing very well indeed and she received very few hits in return. The Maoris had indeed put a good luck charm on her.

After the action I went on board the *New Zealand* and my friend replied to my query of why she was so little damaged with a smile. He pointed to the great inscribed motto on her midship screen, 'Ao-tea-roa' – 'The Great White Cloud'.

Again and again our ships were hitting the Germans and our spotter up on the gun control tower remarked that the *Seydlitz* was blazing fore and aft. She must have been badly hit for great clouds of black smoke billowed away to the east, sparks and flames leaping to the sky.

Suddenly our friend got extremely excited and shouted that the 5th 'battle wagons' were hitting the enemy. The midshipmen joined in to tell us they really were being damaged and we felt proud of this great squadron.

Then, without warning and with dramatic speed, a terrible drama was unfolded before our eyes. Some of us saw it but most people merely felt it. The hard-hitting *Queen Mary* blew up with two tremendous explosions, with an interval of about twelve minutes between. One moment she was proudly firing away with her great guns and hitting *Lützow* with repeated regularity, and then in one devastating blow – exit! She was hit by a full salvo and with a mighty roar the forrard magazines blew up.

There she lay, well over on her starboard beam, her back broken. She had been firing at the *Seydlitz* until that ship's return fire was almost silenced, and then she had switched her accurate gunfire on to the German flagship, *Lützow.* One by one, men could be seen coming out of the after turret and climbing down on to the exposed bilge keel and jumping into the water. Also, rolls and rolls of white paper came streaming out of her after hatch situated on her quarter deck. These must have been spare rolls of Dreyer's chart paper, because her gunnery office was situated close to the after hatch. It went trailing away over the boiling sea like a shaking toilet roll.

When quite a few men were already in the water, the second explosion occurred. A tremendous great black cloud of smoke enveloped our ship. We were steaming next astern of her and it was like going into a Cimmerian cavern. We were completely obscured by the denseness of the smoke and the noise was appalling. Many onlookers thought that we, too, had gone.

Our gunnery officer, with the ship in complete darkness, decided that this was a chance to line up and check the gun director system, which he did in record time, running all electrical instruments to zero and putting on a setting, checking all indicators to see that they were reading correctly. Thanks to Petty Officer Wilton and his staff, they were all correct, the guns reading the same as the master director indicators, not as much as half a degree out.

Suddenly we found ourselves out in broad daylight again, and that vast expanse of smoke was left behind in our wake. Then once again our great guns roared out, but this time they seemed to say 'Revenge!' A friend, 'Nigger' Darke, told me later in Cheltenham that *Tiger* seemed to leap forward from the dark abyss, shake her 'snots' and with a huge snarl and a great bellow from her vindictive main armament, answered the question from *Lion*'s look-out: 'Is she gone?'

The Padre passed through the battery and told us that one of the destroyers was going to pick up the few survivors, and we felt a little better after that. She was a very gallant ship, Cockney-manned from Chatham Barracks, and her Captain was a great skipper, a man with ideas well ahead of his time. He believed in efficiency and the very best for his ship and its company, and in this sad moment we spoke of some of his improvements. She was the first ship in the Navy to have a proper church and her discipline was regulated by ordinary petty officers, the often ham-fisted ship's police being dispensed with. She was indeed sadly missed at that moment.

My friend in the *New Zealand* told me that they had all felt proud of *Lion* and *Tiger* at that moment – Beatty's 'beautiful cats' were padding through a jungle of shell splinters and firing rapid six gun salvos while ignoring the enemy's fire which moved closer. They sped through the forest of disturbed water to snarl with their great guns, creating fearful execution on the battered Germans.

We were now four battle cruisers to the enemy's five, and for a while we were hard pressed, but retribution was creeping up on them in the shape of Evan Thomas. His magnificent Battle Squadron was racing up, roaring defiance, and hitting Hipper's rear battle cruisers time and again.

Suddenly more drama! A great shout from Billy Lowe, our gunlayer, brought us to the slits between the gun shield and the ship's side. Here we could just see the destroyers going into action. I climbed inside the gun shield and the gunlayer slid out of the way.

What a sight met my eyes! Nine destroyers of the 13th Flotilla, *Nestor, Nomad, Narborough, Pelican, Petard, Obdurate* and *Nerissa*, with *Moorsom* and *Morris* of the 10th Flotilla, and with their supporting light cruiser leader, *Champion,* had been ordered out ahead to deliver a torpedo attack. This was soon after Beatty had made his classic remark to his Flag Captain Chatfield: 'What wrong with our b— ships today? Sail two points closer to the enemy.' Then he bit savagely through his third pipe stem.

Away they sped, these slim, grim avengers, steaming at high speed, 32-34 knots, to get into the torpedo-attacking position, ahead and on the bow of the enemy battle cruisers. This caused a similar move on the part of the Germans and we were very thrilled with what we saw. Some time later a poem was published in the *Fleet.* Here is a verse:

White from the salt spray forrard,
Black from the smoke stacks aft,
Bang went the four inch forrard,
And bang went the b— aft.

This was a tremendous thrill. Through the shell-torn waters, with the great guns of both sides firing hell for leather over their heads, in went the little ships of war, and like barking dogs they fired at one another steaming towards and passing each other at the speed of an express train, 60 knots deflection being set on their sights. And, symbolically, the noise of battle had changed and the music of the guns was like some vast orchestra sounding out the notes of Wagner's 'Ride of the Valkyries'.

Right into the jaws of death rode the little ships of war, great plumes of water hissing upwards and boiling all around them as the enemy heavy and light guns fought to keep them at bay. Our friend up top now took up the story. He saw the *Seydlitz* reel out of the line with a great hole torn in her guts, and taking in four thousand tons of water she heeled over to the torpedo damage from one of our destroyers.

Later her Captain, by counter-flooding the other side of the ship, got her low down in the water back on to an even keel.

During this part of the action, the news was flashed by wireless from Commodore Goodenough in *Southampton* that the enemy's Battle Fleet was in sight. This was the most pregnant moment in the whole of the Battle of Jutland, because it meant that if any of our ships lost speed they would become sitting ducks and would be sunk. In addition, we knew that when Beatty reversed his course and swung his ships around to course north, if the enemy followed they would be trapped by our Battle Fleet.

Commander Bingham, VC, hero of many actions, Captain of *Nestor*, a destroyer leader, led a very gallant attack in company with *Nomad* and *Nicator*, converging on to the huge German High Seas Fleet.

Now we had turned an opposite course. Our midshipman up in the gun control tower was talking to our voice pipe friend and he gave us the gist of it, and this is my description of it. 'Here they come, their top masts, a forest of steel posts, marching up over the horizon, like legions of the big battalions' – a poetry of majestic might. Bingham's three destroyers speeding out towards them, were caught in a pillar of shell spouts and rode right through them until at last two lay stopped, disabled, with their engine rooms shot through.

So they drifted, *Nestor* and *Nomad*, dead ducks, lying between the lines of opposing warships. As the German Battle Fleet passed them, the *Nestor* fired her last torpedo, in a final effort of defiance. The Germans poured into them a devastating hail of gunfire and the two destroyers sank beneath the shell-torn waters, with *Nestor* flying her brand new battle ensign before the waters closed over her. We were glad to learn later that the Germans saved many of the crews of these two gallant ships.

Previously the *Nicator*, had on arriving, offered to tow *Nestor* but Bingham waved her on, and later she joined up with *Champion,* answering Beatty's Destroyer Recall signal.

Returning to the destroyer action, the Germans lost at least two destroyers sunk, and they also admitted to the *Seydlitz* being torpedoed in the starboard side. During my post-war duties in the torpedo lecture rooms, I gleaned a great deal of information which makes me think perhaps Jerry lost more ships at Jutland than they admitted.

In the daylight destroyer attacks many a gallant little action went by unnoticed in the fierce melee between the opposing forces. The signals now in the hands of Beatty and Jellicoe heralding the approach of the German High Seas Fleet altered the whole course of the action.

The 'Run to the South' was over.

### *The 'Run to the North'*

When the message was received in *Iron Duke*, Jellicoe immediately issued the general alert signal to Admiralty, who alerted dockyards, hospital ships and shore establishments etc.: 'Fleet Action imminent.' And at Whitehall the War Staff pondered over the huge wall maps and wondered how it would work out.

Beatty's turn to the north was made at the right moment. Even so, for a short while we were the target for the leading German battleships, and great shell spouts spurted all around us, to break at their summit, to cascade, drenching water on our decks and superstructures.

One of our lads became terribly frightened and said, 'We are alone, fighting the whole of the German Navy! We have been thrown to the wolves!'

But he cheered up when we drew out of range with our superior speed. In a short while Hipper did likewise, also turning north. The trap was set. We were leading the whole of the High Seas Fleet into the waiting, hungry guns of the British Grand Fleet, now some sixty-odd miles to the north. The time was then about 4.35 p.m.

Evan Thomas, who was late coming into action with his wonderful battleships, was now slow in turning north. Very gallantly he held on and covered Beatty's retreat. If the German ships were built only to fight in the North Sea, then the ships of the

Queen Elizabeth Class were built to sustain great punishment and fight back with tremendous power.

After sustaining many hits from battle cruisers and battleships of the German High Seas Fleet, they turned and swung magnificently round, course north, with all their guns blazing death and defiance to Von Scheer's Fleet just coming up over the horizon and walking into Jellicoe's trap. Admittedly, *Warspite*'s after turret roof top was rocking like a broken saucer, exposing her gun crew working their guns like Trojans of old. Beatty's squadron's speed now started to draw Hipper's battered battle cruisers away from the safety of Von Scheer's battleships, and now gun after gun of Hipper's stricken ships fell silent, some from the want of targets and some silent in death, their crews gone to meet their Maker.

Our destroyers had put on their top speed to keep ahead of Beatty and his ships and they followed their cruiser swanlike leaders, like cygnets on a disturbed lake with great bow waves breaking away from their curving forefronts creaming away in their wakes. This now became the 5th Battle Squadron's finest hour, their great guns fiercely mangling the upper works of the leading German ships, and with their superior speed and gun range they were able to fight and out-manoeuvre the enemy. I will describe this later.

We received several further hits and our armoured steel split open like brittle pea-pods, but nothing of any consequence. Suddenly however the ship lurched and we felt the deck heave beneath us, and in our gun casement the rammer tub slid across the deck, kissed the stacked shells like a curtsey, and slid back again. Then the *Tiger* righted herself and steamed on at the speed of the Fleet.

Later I remarked to our Battery Officer, 'Cargo Bill', that we must have had a big hit just then. He replied, 'Nothing much, Hayward, a shell in the after forecastle deck. Go up and get some Woodbines out of the dry goods canteen. It's been knocked out and the Stoker Fire Party will only ruin them with their hoses.'

My Captain of the Gun nodding his agreement, I ran up to the after forecastle deck. Complete chaos met my eyes. An 11 inch shell had exploded on the deck and started a small fire, and a huge ghastly hole gaped at me through which one could have driven a bus. The door tilted crazily and seemed to grim like a toothless old woman. The canteen looked like the Wreck of the Hesperus. I salvaged a box of Woodbines and then stepped through where the door had previously been, and out on to the upper deck. Away in the distance I saw the magnificent 5th Battle Squadron.

We were only firing occasionally now but the great battleships, with their much greater range, were hard at it, huge orange flashes bursting from their gun barrels. Then came the booming violence of their angry velocity. Sometimes they were walled from my view by fantastic fountains of shell splashes, only to emerge still firing their ponderous guns. It seemed they were immune to Jerry's shellfire. From deck level I could not see the German ships and I was too scared to go up on to the 'booms'. I could tell that although the enemy was superior in numbers our boys were more than holding their own. Our heavier guns and greater speed were telling the tale.

This was a splendid rearguard action that Evan Thomas was fighting and his wonderful ships were well equipped for this titanic struggle. Besides the very best in 15 inch guns, with the extreme range of 25,000 yards, they were able to hit the enemy, their gunnery being extremely good. They had the very best and latest up-to-date Dreyer mechanical and electrical computers, which eliminated every error except human error in the firing of these massive guns.

In ignorance the enemy pursued us, not realising that Jellicoe was steaming now at 20 knots away southward to meet them head on. At 18 knots and with a relative speed of nearly 38 knots, they steamed to disaster at the speed of an express train. Jerry was being lured to death and destruction.

Now our paymaster came into our gun casement and told us the number of hits we had received, that is, major hits. The minor damage was not considered by anyone. Later, our gunnery officer told us that our target mostly during the battle cruiser action was a ship with a red band on her centre funnel; this we knew later to have been the *Derfflinger*.

At 4.50 p.m. we were back on our tracks where the *Indefatigable* had blown up. It seemed as if a wind from heaven had blown away all traces of that terrible destruction. The waters were clear.

Beatty, by putting on speed, had drawn too far ahead and we suddenly found ourselves out of range. We were invited to go on deck for a breather. I went up with our gunners to have a look at 'Q' turret. I could see she had had a very nasty hit and the right gun hanging at a curious angle of depression which gave the turret a hangdog look, the barrel almost touching the deck.

Suddenly a great cheer went up. A destroyer passed us, coming from the south-west and steaming under our starboard quarter as she swept past us, going like a bomb, with an enormous hole in her guts, her great black action ensign tattered and soot-stained, shook and trembled, black from the smoke stacks aft. We watched her coxswain poke his head out of the wheel house and with a wave of the hand acknowledge our cheers, then with two long blasts on the siren, the gallant little ship turned to port and away she sped with sparks and smoke belching from her shell-shot funnels, sounding and looking for all the world like 'Casey Jones' and the 'Cannonball Express'. She was probably the *Petard*, having stopped to pick up the few survivors from the *Queen Mary*. Away she swept, a dramatic sight, having fired all her torpedoes at the enemy and much of her 4 inch ammunition, hurrying to rejoin her flotilla leader, *Champion*.

Just then we all scattered back to our action stations: the firing had broken out again. We and the enemy exchanged a few shots; the visibility was growing poor, a sort of light mist descending on the waters.

During the time between 5.00 and 6.00 p.m. was perhaps our easiest period during the major part of the action.

Beatty now eased the speed of the Fleet to 24 knots to get back into range. The distance between us and the enemy decreased and soon the dim outlines of the German ships became visible to our rangetakers. At 14,000 yards we opened fire again and our gunnery officer reported that we were continually hitting the enemy. Jerry's firing now became spasmodic, a round here and there, and very much out of range. We realised now that we did not have a great deal to fear from Hipper's battle cruisers.

At about 5.30 p.m. there was another lull in the action. This time we did not go up on deck but sat around smoking and listening to Evan Thomas and his 'battle wagons' dishing it out.

Suddenly the enemy ran into a clearer patch and Hipper's ships stood out stark and naked to the tremendous fire from our guns; all our heavies were firing except the right gun of Q and, of course, the *Lion*'s midship turret was silent, with smoke still pouring through the roof. The remainder of our Squadron could still fire most of their main armament guns. *Princess Royal* also had her Y turret knocked out.

Beatty was now transmitting all his wireless signals to Jellicoe

## APPROXIMATE POSITIONS DURING THE RUN TO THE NORTH: 4.35- 8 p.m. APPROXIMATELY

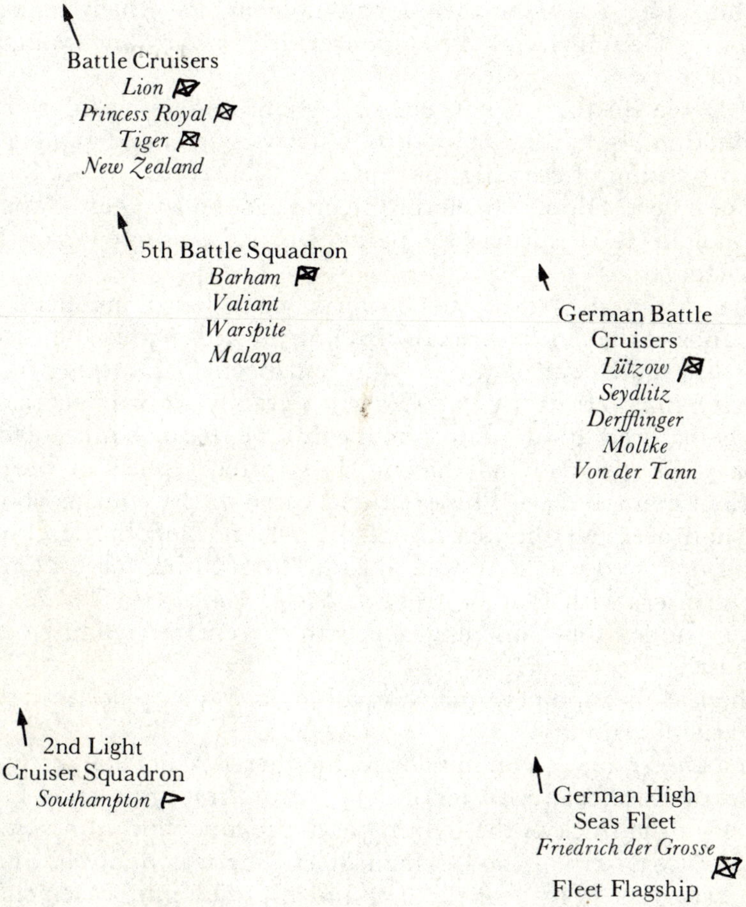


*This rough sketch is intended only to give an idea of the Course of the Action.*

through *Princess Royal*, as *Lion*'s main aerial had been shot away.

On receipt of the signal 'Enemy in sight', Jellicoe had dispatched to our aid the Hon. Horace Hood, the Admiral in charge of the 3rd Battle Cruiser Squadron, flying his Flag in *Invincible*. With her two consorts, *Inflexible* and *Indomitable*, they worked up to their top speed and raced southwards at 27 knots to meet and help us.

Our Grand Fleet had now worked up to their topmost speed of 21 knots and were awaiting the deployment signal from the flagship. This was now their great moment, for which Jellicoe's Admirals, Captains and crews had trained so hard and waited so long for.

Sir David Beatty was now edging his four remaining ships of the 1st and 2nd Squadrons on a north-easterly course, and gaining the envied position of crossing the enemy's 'T' and our smoke hiding Jellicoe's fleet. Hipper was forced to give ground and our 'Gunnery Jack' told us later this was the period when *Tiger* scored many hits on her target.

The 'Run to the North' was now nearing its hard fought end and the hands of the clock were now coming towards 6 p.m. Our friend up in the gun control tower, who had been rather quiet lately, reported that Jerry's fire had slackened greatly, only an occasional shot being fired at our ship. About this time, Rear-Admiral Hood, in *Invincible*, decided that having no sighting reports of Beatty's position, conferred with his staff and came to the conclusion that they had overshot the bearing of the 1st and 2nd Battle Cruiser Squadrons, and was now well ahead. His scouting forces, *Chester*, light cruiser, with four destroyers, *Shark, Christopher, Ophelia* and *Acasta*, suddenly became engaged with the enemy looming out of the mist.

Then at that moment many small actions took place, owing to the variable visibility.

The *Chester*, newly commissioned and therefore not worked up for battle practice, came in for a very rough time. She soon found herself in the thick of the fighting and at cannonade with some of the finest cruisers of the German Fleet. She was badly hit, her 6 inch batteries being raked fore and aft, her gun casements a shambles, but she did her best and fought on. Boy 1st Class Cornwall posthumously won a Victoria Cross from the action. Mortally wounded, he continued to give out the orders he received through his voice pipe to his sorely-pressed comrades. Eventually he sank to the blood-stained deck among the dead and dying of his gun's crew, a gallant end.

Commander Loftus Jones led his destroyer flotilla out against the German battle cruisers, to deliver a torpedo attack. Although heavily outnumbered by the opposing German light forces, he fought heroically with satanic fury until the German cruiser *Regensburg* came to their rescue, hitting *Shark* in the engine room with a well-placed shell.

The thrust of the *Shark*'s propellers died away and Loftus Jones found his little ship stopped and marooned in the midst of the enemy. He fought on until all his guns were shot away and he himself had been mortally wounded, both legs severed by gunfire. Almost his last dying words were an order to hoist a new ensign at the 'gaff', to replace the black shred of the old one. Soon his gallant little ship sank beneath the lapping waves and he drifted away to death at the bottom of the water in a Carley Float.

Loftus Jones was awarded a posthumous Victoria Cross, richly earned, and the gallant *Shark* in death was not alone. Almost the last round fired from her midship gun caused one of the German 'V' class destroyers to join the graveyard of sunken ships in the sullen waters of the Jutland Bank.

Our light forces, being so outnumbered, fell back on to the support of Hood and his battle cruisers; although we had lost *Shark* the Germans had also had their losses and now the 3rd Battle Cruiser Squadron, Hood's 'Merry Men', came blazing into action. A full salvo of 12 inch shells from *Invincible* stopped the German *Wiesbaden* dead in her tracks, a drifting hulk in a few moments, while the remainder of the squadron hit *Regensburg* and she limped away into the mist with one boiler room out of action.

This part of the fight at Jutland is known to Naval historians as the action at 'Windy Corner'.

Now began the greatest cannonade in the naval history of the world.

Jellicoe had now received rather second-hand reports from Goodenough, Sinclair and Beatty, still away to the south, to enable him with some certainty to deploy his vast fleet into line of battle. This moment was pregnant with uncertainty. Was the reported position of the enemy the true position? Would they emerge from the east or the west? At last, a signal lamp flashing an 'enemy position' message from *Lion* as she appeared out of the haze put

Jellicoe's mind at rest. He had been right in his estimation of the true position of the High Seas Fleet of Von Scheer. A slighter alteration of course, and at the given signal Jellicoe's mighty fleet of twenty-four super-Dreadnoughts swung slowly into battle array and the great battleships began to string out into a vast crescendo which straightened out into a lop-sided, awe-inspiring L.

For Jellicoe and his captains this was the moment of truth, for they now began to perceive a forest of masts appearing out of the mists, and these of course must be German. Yes, Jellicoe like Beatty had achieved that great dream of all admirals – to 'cross the enemy's "T" ', in which all his ships could fire their broadsides while the enemy could only fire their foremost guns.

At this moment I must pause a little and return to a previous point in my story.

*Invincible*, going back to link up with Beatty and the main battle cruisers, came across *Lion* and formed their line of battle ahead of Beatty's ships and, in Beatty's own words in the action report, 'Came magnificently into action'.

Our friend up in the gun control tower saw them arrive and swing around ahead of us, their great long barrelled 12 inch guns spitting death and destruction to the enemy battle cruisers. The time was just after 6 p.m. He shouted out a running commentary of their daring nearness to the German ships. Yes, it was fresh ships and fresh gunners coming to our aid and we were thrilled to see them steaming proudly into action. It was like new blood through our veins. We had been over two hours in action and, except for two short periods, had had to fight hard all the way. We were greatly cheered to see them; we felt our nerves, which had been stretched like bowstrings, begin to relax.

Horace Hood's new course was making the third leg of a triangle and we now got the running commentary from the gun control tower personnel. The gunnery of the 3rd Battle Cruiser Squadron was tremendous in its majestic intensity. Hits were showing all over Hipper's battle cruisers, great rippling salvos running down the line of our three 12 inch gunned consorts, as they steamed through the shell-torn waters with the range closing all the time. At 14,000 yards and less they were doing fearful execution to the enemy's ships.

All this punishment continued until Lieutenant Commander Halse, gunnery officer of the *Derfflinger*, gravely perplexed by the terrible damage to his squadron, decided to have one last throw of the dice. Turning to his personal servant and senior rangetaker, he asked for the range of the British flagship. Then, with only two guns left in action, he blew up *Invincible* with a thunderous roar and a sheet of flame shot up straight from the orbs of Hell. Once again the hand of Fate scythed against the light cavalry of the Fleet and another battle cruiser died. A magazine explosion in her midship turret made her a flaming holocaust with death to almost her entire crew. Her back was broken completely into two separate parts.

Soon after the action we were told by an officer how Horace Hood was congratulating the gunnery officer up in the spotting top by means of the bridge voice pipe. He was saying that every round was going home. Suddenly, his life was snuffed out like a candle. This same gunnery commander just stepped from the drunken listing spotting top on to the wooden battens of a Mark IV Target which had drifted off the booms as she sank. When picked up by the destroyer *Badger*, he was quite dry-shod and unconcerned, then told the story of the Admiral's praise for the ship's gunnery.

Shortly after she blew up I saw her through our gun ports with my own eyes, the two ends sticking out of the water looking for all the world like the dorsal fins of a great shark. We all cheered, but suddenly we stopped.

Our gunlayer, Billy Lowe, said in a low voice breaking with heart-felt intensity, 'Dry up, you bastards,' as he looked through his telescope. 'I was out in the Straits in the *Queen* and that was our "chummy ship", the *Invincible*. She was our "chummy ship" and was always painted that colour.'

Suddenly our trainer said, 'You are right, Bill, I can read her name on the stern. It's painted out all right but it's the *Invincible*.' He could see through the high-powered lens of his telescope.

You may wonder why the two ends were sticking out of the water so motionless. Off the coast of Jutland, the depth of water is 25 to 30 fathoms deep and the sunken battle cruiser was roughly 600 feet long, that is, 6 feet to a fathom. This explains why her two ends were so far out of the water.

We turned sadly away from the gun ports and for the third time that day felt the full horror of this terrible action. But retribution was at hand, and the mighty guns of Jellicoe's Battle Fleet began to sound their drums of death along the battle line. Scouting all well ahead of the Grand Fleet was Admiral Sir Robert Arbuthnot's

GRAND FLEET DEPLOYING 6.0-6.30 p.m.

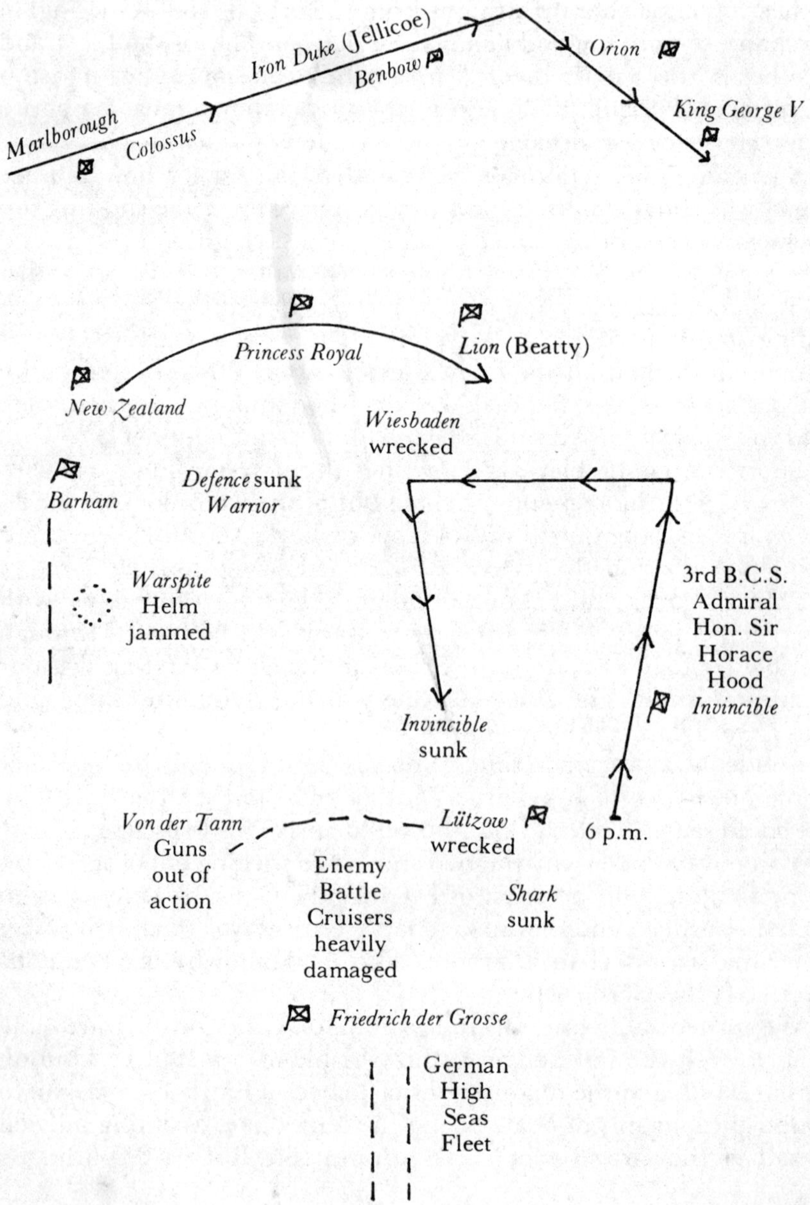

squadron of armoured cruisers, flagship *Defence, Black Prince, Warrior* and *Duke of Edinburgh.* These ships were modern armoured cruisers and mounted four 9.2 inch and ten 7.5 guns, the best of the heavy gunned cruisers of that era. Scouting well ahead of Jellicoe's line of ships they pressed forward with great impatience, steaming to the sound of the guns.

Sir Robert always told his officers and men that he would stop at nothing to help Jellicoe, his great commander-in-chief, who was a particular friend of his. He steamed forward past the British battle cruisers in great haste to get at grips with the enemy, and to signal back their course and speed. As it turned out, helping Jellicoe was exactly what he did.

Out of the mist loomed the almost helpless *Wiesbaden*, stopped, but not quite dead, in her tracks because her after gun spoke and the British cruisers swung into action against her. It has been said that cruisers are hard to die and this German certainly was.

Our lad in the gun control tower then told us that the British armoured cruisers were smothering her and with their intership firing, great fountains of water hiding the *Wiesbaden* from sight. Everyone seeing her thought she must sink at any moment. Bobby Arbuthnot did not stop to watch the results of the effect of his ship's gunfire but pressed gallantly on. Then out of the south appeared a forest of masts, many units of the German Fleet barring his path. He had run into their guns and these were to prove his utter ruin.

Nothing daunted, Sir Robert went straight into action with his celebrated inter-ship firing, in which all ships fired their guns as if the guns belonged to one ship instead of to four. There was, however, only one end to such a struggle. The German heavy units leapt into action. The gunfire was terrible to watch and the flagship *Defence*, being the British leading ship, caught the first salvos. Eye witnesses say that she seemed to stop and a cloud of coal dust came up above her upper decks, then she picked up and steamed proudly on, still firing her guns.

Then came the end. A little later more shells rained down on the stricken vessel, followed swiftly by a tremendous explosion, which was heard by nearly everyone on both sides of the battle line. I can hear that sound now. For a moment everyone who saw the event stopped at the sight. She blew sky high, her picket boat performing a giant Catherine wheel right above a gigantic mushroom cloud of flame and smoke. It was a stunning and frightful sight and our friend whispered down the voice pipe, 'Oh my God, what a sight!' He had had a ringside seat that day.

The *Duke of Edinburgh* made a violent 'alter course' and steamed away to the north-west and safety, but the *Warrior* and *Black Prince* would have died there and then had it not been for an extraordinary incident, which rescued them from the dreadful nightmare of the moment. Up from the south-west in dramatic action came the 5th Battle Squadron, still methodically firing their great guns at any target that loomed in their sights.

Suddenly at that moment the *Warspite*'s helm jammed and for the *Warrior*'s ship's company this was the most critical moment in the entire action. Immediately the Germans shifted target and poured their tremendous fire on to the *Warspite*, thinking that they could repeat their performance. However, not a bit of it! She went skidding round like a Plymouth bus on an ice patch and performed two or three great complete circles, surrounded all the time by mountainous shell splashes. Great spouts of water hid her from view. Captain Phillimore and his crew worked desperately to free the steering gear and by using her engines succeeded in making out a course which suddenly freed the rudder. She steamed proudly away, still firing her full heavy complement of 15 inch guns.

She should have died during these desperate turns but the wonderful workmanship and good British armour more than saved the ship. She lived to fight and to fight gallantly in the Second World War. No wonder she became known with affection as the 'Grand Old Lady'. On she steamed, still raking the Germans fore and aft with her terrible gunfire. Slowly at first, looking like a belated cross-channel packet, all smoke and no steam, trying to make the morning tide, then working up to her full speed to join up with her consorts away to the north-west, taking her place in the main line of battle.

Sad to say, however, both armoured cruisers *Warrior* and *Black Prince* were doomed. *Warrior* was taken in tow by that maid of all work the carrier *Engadine*, only to be abandoned next morning; she sank somewhere in the centre of the North Sea, her crew standing stiffly to attention at the pipe 'Still', to allow the wounded to be transferred across the pitching, corkscrewing ship to safety, both vessels grinding steel against steel as the two Captains, with superb seamanship, held the two ships together.

It was here that Flight Lieutenant Rutland RN earned and won the Albert Gold Medal. A seaman from the sinking *Warrior* fell into the sea and was calling for help between the bows of the two ships. Rutland bent on a bowline and dived overboard to save the man with the same skill and *sangfroid* that allowed him to scout up in the skies the previous afternoon.

I will return to the story of the *Black Prince* later, and the manner in which I came to hear it.

Just after 6.10 p.m. Jellicoe completed his deployment. The deployment and the actions at 'Windy Corner' were one great drama rapidly unfolding, so rapidly indeed that parts of this gigantic battle are told out of proportion to what actually happened.

Sir John knew that at this moment he could lose the entire war. Britain could be invaded and as a nation we could cease to exist. It was a moment pregnant with historical significance, a war game of chess. One false move would result in the cry of 'Mate!'

It is necessary to remember that Jellicoe had to range his battle line of twenty-four battleships from the five divisions they were stationed in to a long line by squadrons, seven miles in length with, of course, the 5th Battle Squadron steaming hard up from the south and, as we know, very much in action. Beatty had to take up his battle station in front, which was also over a mile in length, and with the light cruisers and destroyers the entire line was some twelve miles long.

Von Scheer was still steaming north and congratulating himself on catching what he thought were isolated squadrons of the British Fleet. Suddenly out of the mist he saw Jellicoe's vast Fleet arranged in battle deployment. As he himself described it in his dispatches, 'I was held in an awful ring of steel.' Our battleships loomed up out of the smoke like threatening giants spewing death and destruction.

Hipper himself was the first to realise, and to see the terrible truth of his Commander-in-Chief's massive blunder. Hard on his heels Von Scheer realised his impending doom. The great long arms of the British Fleet stretched out like a frightful yawning chasm of flaming steel, about to engulf him and his much-vaunted High Seas Fleet.

The Germans felt and saw the tremendous might of that fearful cannonade, the like of which no man will ever hear again. The British steel-clad monsters were bearing down upon them, all available guns blazing away, with the terrible sight of ships like the

*Agincourt*, with her full broadside of seven turrets, fourteen 12 inch guns, all firing together, her forest of guns elevated like the branches of some great tree, erupting flame and steel. They moved through the battle smoke like monsters from another world. Our gunnery officer told us later it was appalling, and salvo after ripped and burst on the leading ships of the German Fleet. A tremendous avalanche of explosive battered their armour in as though it had been made of tinplate.

Jellicoe's huge crescent of battleships into which Von Scheer was steaming would soon have spelled his utter ruin. However, before I continue with that part of the narrative, I must tell you that we too came across the remains of the *Wiesbaden*. As her colours were still flying it meant that she had not surrendered and therefore was a menace. At 4,000 yards we poured into her a devastating fire from our starboard 6 inch guns. We were glad to be firing. We in our battery had been out of range throughout the action and we knew that she could still fire in return her torpedoes from submerged tubes.

We smothered her with a torrent of rapid independent fire and it was possible to see our lyddite shells bursting all over her. She was now a smoking hulk, a gallant little cruiser. We passed on and she must have been engaged by scores of British ships and hit by every type of shell made at Woolwich Arsenal.

Eventually she was engaged and torpedoed by Captain Tovey (later to become British Commander-in-Chief in the Second World War) in the *Onslow*. *Onslow* was returning from a torpedo attack and, although disabled, only able to steam at fifteen knots; Captain Tovey altered course and fired his last torpedo into the dying *Wiesbaden*. But – and I say but – most naval historians consider that it was *Wiesbaden* that torpedoed the *Marlborough*, the only British battleship to suffer from a torpedo hit in the whole of the action. The historians consider that it was her last act of defiance before she drifted off the scene of the battle. A German destroyer tried to rescue the gallant remains of her crew, but was driven off by the accurate gunfire of units of the British Fleet. Her chief stoker was the sole survivor who lived to tell of the Homeric end of this brave little cruiser.

He was found drifting on a raft nearly three days later by a Swedish vessel, nursed back to health and returned to Germany.

The awful cannonade of British fire continued. It was

stupendous, the noise deafening and it seemed as though we were continually being hit about the ears with no relief. Our friends in the gun control tower were quiet now. They could not hear themselves speak.

Jellicoe's brilliant manoeuvre had certainly caught Von Scheer's Fleet in what seemed an inescapable trap, but with Teutonic thoroughness he ordered his Fleet to retire. It was a signal which virtually ordered them to escape if they could. At the same time, he ordered his destroyers to attack. Scheer could not actually see the British ships at that moment, only the bright orange flashes of their terrible guns, whilst coming out of the mist they appeared to the British gunners clear, stark and naked. With renewed fury, Jellicoe's director layers fired 15 inch, 13.5 inch and 12 inch guns, all roaring out together, and then our spotting officers saw the German destroyers coming out to attack us. At the same time, we saw Von Scheer's battleships turning away and starting to run like a herd of frightened elephants. How they managed to avoid colliding with each other is a mystery to all who witnessed the debacle. Our gunners just fired into the 'brown' as they blundered this way and that, sirens hooting, engines churning the steel grey waters to foaming white in their frenzy to escape from the explosive British hell.

Beatty saw the destroyers coming in to attack and every possible gun on our side poured a devastating fire on to the tiny torpedo craft. This was our golden moment! We were jubilant as the sound of the secondary armament guns turned the music of the battle to a sort of staccato thunder, which sent the sound waves churning in our ears.

They told us later that our friend in the gun control tower was tremendously elated with all he saw and was jumping up and down with excitement. I know the gunlayers were all claiming to have sunk such-and-such a German destroyer. More than one was caught by a deluge of bursting shells and turned completely turtle. The enemy destroyers fired their torpedoes in haste and these missiles barely reached our lines. They were easily avoided as they slowly reached the end of their range, with their propellers only just turning.

The *Marlborough* was hit aft by a torpedo but I have already stated that the naval historians have claimed that it was fired by *Wiesbaden*. *Marlborough* held her place in the line, her guns still

VON SCHEER'S GREATEST BLUNDER, AND THE UNAVAILING CHARGE OF THE GERMAN LIGHT BRIGADE

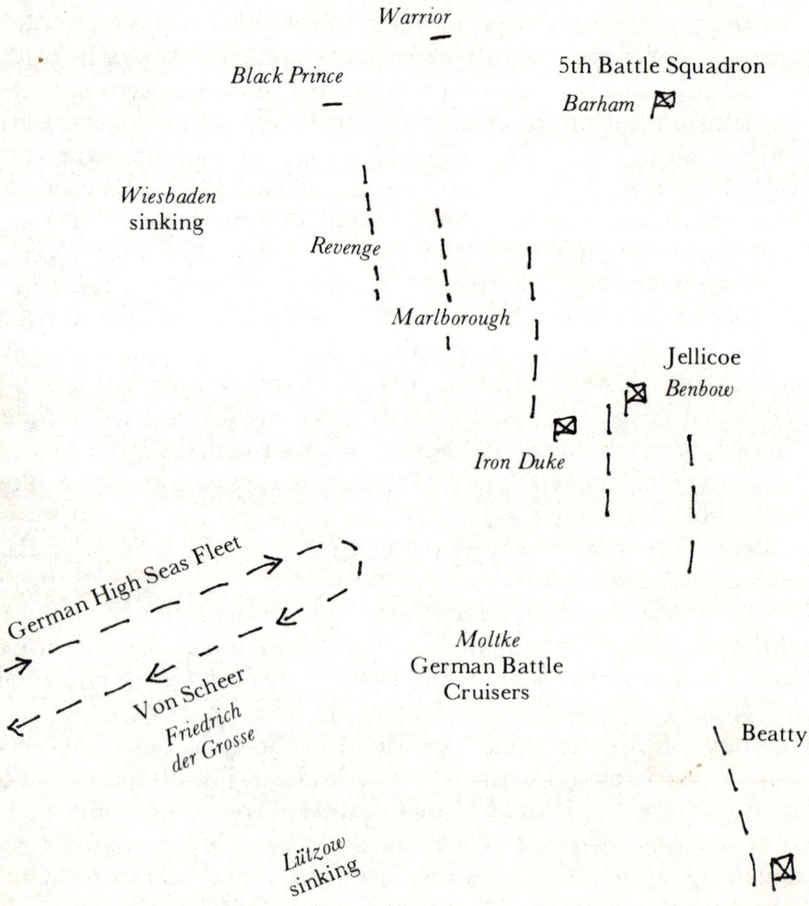

firing, and did not leave the Fleet until about 11.30 p.m. that night. The firing gradually died away as the German Fleet scrambled off away to the south-west. A peaceful hush fell on the shell-torn waters and gradually our hammered ears began to take in sounds again. Even in the quietness we wondered when the battle would recommence.

The time was now just before 7 p.m. and our outposts were soon searching for the enemy in the darkening mist. Commodores Sinclair and Goodenough were scanning the dense horizons for sight of our stricken foe.

The German battle cruisers were now in a very bad way. Their flagship *Lützow* could not fire a shot and was slowly sinking; she just drifted off the battlefield. During the early part of the action she had been repeatedly hit by *Lion* during the 'Run to the South', and by *Malaya* during the 'Run to the North'. Also Horace Hood's close range action had paid a dividend. Yes, her position had become hopeless. Hipper left his flagship and with the remains of her crew boarded a destroyer away from the dreadful nightmare of the moment.

Jellicoe eventually got a rough bearing on the enemy and altered course to the westward. Then Von Scheer made his second great blunder. Thinking that if he steamed due east his ships would pass astern of the British Fleet, he altered course to the eastward, hoping that he could escape that way and get between the British Fleet and home.

Once more the awful apparition of the Royal Navy in battle array steamed across their path with all guns blazing, as they tried to escape towards Germany. Once again Jellicoe was crossing Von Scheer's 'T'.

Scheer's leading ships took a fearful hammering and reeled from the onslaught of the devastating British fire. The German commander, in desperation, made his now famous signal to Captain Hartog, the new battle cruiser commander in *Derfflinger*: 'At The Enemy Charge.' The *Derfflinger* and her consorts swung into the jaws of death, to steam straight into the lines of the British ships to ram them, and would have died there and then. For a few minutes they withstood the onslaught of the full fury of the nearest British battleships. This Ride of the Valkyries was sheer suicide. The havoc created in those already severely damaged German battle cruisers was appalling, and had it not been for the presence of mind of the dashing leader of the German destroyers, who once more ordered his light craft to attack, Jellicoe's battleships would have brought about the end of the German Fleet.

There were still a good two hours of daylight left and a great deal could still happen in that time.

Once more Jellicoe ordered a 'Turn away'. This was at that time the expected and prudent thing to do.

The German light forces went into the attack and Captain Hartog turned his ships parallel to the British lines, hiding behind a smoke screen. This saved that once proud squadron that had fought so well from certain destruction. However, they were no longer a fighting unit, mere battered hulks, and later Von Scheer ordered them home, if this were possible.

When the German destroyers attacked, it seemed to the onlookers that the British gunfire simply massacred the tiny boats that steamed towards them. The survivors fired their few torpedoes and turned about, fleeing from that hurricane of bursting shells, leaving one destroyer leader stopped dead in her tracks. Later, when the smoke of battle had cleared, this German destroyer leader could be seen to be still floating with her flag still flying, so *Obedient, Mindful, Marvel* and *Onslaught* closed in to finish her with torpedoes, which they promptly did.

Once again Von Scheer turned his ships away to the north-west, away from the British Fleet's attack, and Hipper coming up in a destroyer started the hopeless task of looking for a good battle cruiser in which to hoist his flag. The *Seydlitz* was now just a floating hulk, all guns shot away, very low in the water, bows almost under, a mass of flame and smoke. Strangely enough, however, she was still able to steam slowly. The *Derfflinger* was not much better off. She was certainly not a fighting unit any longer. The *Von Der Tann* could still steam but whether she could have fired a gun is doubtful; her upper works seemed a mass of twisted steel. Eventually Hipper settled for the acting flagship *Moltke* and joined up with Captain Hartog. The ship could steam well and fire a couple of light guns, if required.

Our light cruisers did some very good work roughly between eight and nine p.m., scouting for the enemy 180° to the westward around the Grand Fleet. Although the evening was getting quite dark, due to lowering skies, there was still hope that the main antagonists might yet clash again in battle. The mist in places was

*Right* The destruction of HMS *Invincible* as seen from HMS *Inflexible,* five hundred yards astern of her

The wreck of HMS *Invincible.* This photograph was taken from HMS *Benbow* about half an hour after the ship blew up

The surrender of the German Fleet

The *Markgraf, Grosser Kurfurst, Konig Albert, Von der Tann* and *Bayern*

On board HMS *Tiger.* Note aircraft on Q turret

very patchy like old maids' muslin and it was partly due to this that once again many small actions took place.

Our light cruisers ran into our old antagonists, the pitiable wrecks of the German Battle Cruiser Squadron, and with their 6 inch guns raked them fore and aft. Being almost unable to return the fire, except for a few light secondary armament guns, the Germans once more suffered badly.

Rear-Admiral Napier, *Falmouth,* with *Yarmouth* and *Southampton*, besides battering away at them with full salvos of 6 inch, also claimed to have torpedoed the *Derfflinger*. The Germans took almost unbelievable punishment. Their upper decks were swept clean, many upper works going overboard as if some gigantic broom was sweeping them to destruction.

Just after 8 p.m. Beatty submitted a signal to Jellicoe that the Grand Fleet should follow him, so that the main fleets might come once more into action. Accordingly, Jellicoe dispatched Admiral Sir Doveton Sturdee and his squadron of modern battleships, but it was not to be. By 8.30 p.m. it had become a game of blind man's bluff, and we had to give up the hope of renewing the fight that evening.

And Beatty's battle cruisers with their magic names seemed to leap forward, while once again the blazing guns heralded a new death on the dark, satanic waters of the Jutland Bank. We in the battle cruisers came once more into action with a German squadron of pre-Dreadnought battleships. The time was exactly 8.20 p.m. I had just come down from a quick look around the port side of the upper deck, but candidly I could only see our own ships cruising through the dark waters, still searching for the enemy.

These German battleships, all masts and funnels, were soon encountered and our friend in the gun control tower told us that our gunnery officer claimed to have hit one of these 'Heligoland' ships several times. This was good shooting in the poor light. The action lasted about twenty minutes, with a close range of about 10,000 yards, and less. Then they disappeared north-west into the darkness beyond the gloomy horizon, like burning haystacks being hosed out. Before the action ended, the distance had fallen to some 7,000 yards and our port battle of 6 inch guns were attacking fiercely. Then the cease-fire gongs clanged out their clear message of halt, and the last two burning ships were seen no more, hidden by the dark night and the smoke of battle.

At 9 p.m. it was quite dark and looking through the gunlayer's position I saw a solitary masthead light accidentally burning from one of our ships away out to starboard, giving away to the enemy our course and speed.

Jellicoe now placed his ships in the night defence disposition. His main force was well to the east of the Germans and well placed to resume the action at daylight. At roughly 2.30 a.m. the following morning it should be light enough to restart. However, Von Scheer was determined, come hell or high water, to break through and get home well clear of Jellicoe, and so refuse action with his vastly superior foe. It meant breaking through our light forces to the northward and rear of the British lines of heavy ships.

*Night Action 9 p.m. 31st May to 2.30 a.m. 1st June*

It was assumed that the Germans were some fifteen to twenty miles to the westward of the British Fleet.

Just after the Grand Fleet had gone to their Night Defence stations, Admiral Sir Cecil Burney with the 1st Battle Squadron sighted a line of heavy ships to the westward, and doubting their identity he hesitated to fire. Soon they melted away into the darkness. Probably it was Hipper's battered battle cruisers trying to make their way home, although in no position to fight through.

It is a known fact that Von Scheer had to insist later that his admirals and captains force their way through the British lines at all costs. So it was, that after 9 p.m. that night until the first signs of dawn crept up from the east, many small actions took place, fierce and very violent fighting with no quarter asked for and none given. So close were these minor actions that at least on one occasion that old Nelsonian cry went up: 'Stand by to repel boarders!' In the destroyers, cutlasses were reached down from the gun bulkheads' racks.

The following story was related by the torpedo firing officer of the *Southampton*, who joined *Tiger* in 1917, and this is my version of his exciting story.

At 9.15 p.m. while it was still twilight, to the westward the 2nd Light Cruiser Squadron found themselves involved in a sharp, short action in which the *Southampton* claimed to have sunk at least one destroyer. It was obvious that these German light forces were probing from the west to break through to the east and home to the safety of their own minefields.

ROUGH PLAN OF POSITION OF GRAND FLEET 9.0 p.m. 31st MAY

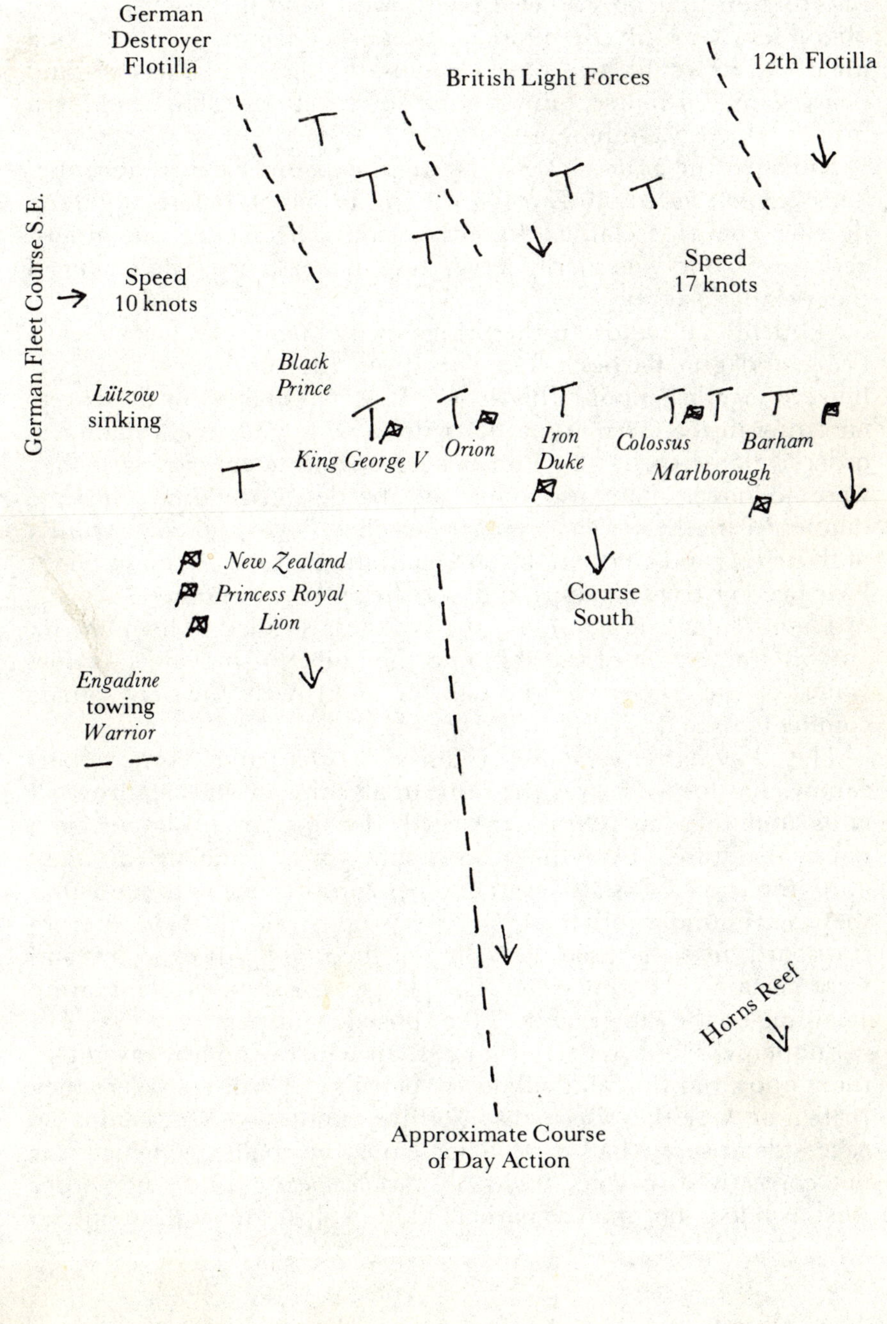

It has been said that that solitary burning masthead light that I and thousands more saw about 9 p.m. gave Von Scheer the information that he was well to the west, and it must have been alight for quite fifteen minutes, because I heard people talking about it. It would give the Germans the speed of the ship and bearing and, of course, quite a good guess that that ship would be a unit of Jellicoe's Grand Fleet.

Anyhow, the *Southampton*'s first night encounter ended abruptly. The enemy faded away into the misty night before anything decisive could be claimed by either side. The silence was almost eerie; everyone was alert, nerves tingling with the excitement of that dramatic affray.

Suddenly all hands on the bridge of the *Nottingham* heard heavy firing and gun flashes coming up from the south-west. No one, however, could pinpoint this action. It was probably our destroyers engaging in the German battle cruisers who, you recall, had been ordered home earlier by Von Scheer, owing to the fact that they were no longer of any use to him as a battle-worthy unit. The time difference in the various reports which I have studied carefully, both British and German, lead me to think that the Germans might have become trigger-happy and were firing at one another.

Then silence fell again and the darkness seemed to hem one in. Just the movement of the ship and the quiet swish of steel against water, as the cruiser slid through the night, were the only sounds coming to us.

The Paymaster's staff produced cocoa and corned beef sandwiches for us. It was the same in all ships in the squadron, all guns and torpedo tubes were ready for instant firing; using a nautical phrase, 'Everything on a split yarn.' Suddenly at 10.20 p.m., the 2nd LCS *Southampton* and her consorts began to sense that they were under observation; everyone strained their eyes to starboard, into the deep dark blue of the night. All expected and were certain that somewhere not far away a ship, or ships, were steaming on the same course. Men spoke in whispers.

Suddenly, like a reflection in a shop window on a foggy night, there appeared the faint silhouette of a line of cruisers. Were they British or were they Germans? For five minutes we kept company, each side unsure what to do. Then came the challenge, which was not correctly answered. Suddenly *Southampton* gave a brisk order (just as a look-out man remarked, 'These blokes must have tiptoed out of the night; we didn't hear a sound.') and the white blinding beam of a searchlight split the darkness and turned the nearest phantom into something real. The light revealed it to be a cruiser of the German Stettin Class and the British flagship revealed her own identity and paid dearly for it, a classic example of the faults of action searchlights. The first was so close one felt one could almost shake hands with the enemy.

Both squadrons fired at opposite numbers and the din was appalling after the quietness of the night, owing to the short range shells travelling high and hitting guns and upper works on both attacked and attacker. It was sharp, fierce, thrust and parry, and we won. The torpedo officer of the *Southampton* saw his chance and immediately seized it. Firing the starboard submerged torpedo tube and the 21 inch 'tinfish' sinking in, it exploded in the guts of the attacker. A wall of flame spread up her shipside and she reeled and staggered out of the enemy line. Later the Germans admitted that she sank.

The gunfire on both sides slackened. Many killed and wounded were strewn around the decks. Eventually, after what seemed an eternity but was actually only a few minutes, the Germans melted away into the black of the night and the action abruptly ended.

The *Nottingham, Birmingham* and *Yarmouth* did not burn searchlights and consequently their action damage was very much less. They claimed, however, to have severely hit and sunk at least one ship.

The night action fighting was the quickest and fiercest in the whole of the Battle of Jutland. No one could tell the whole story and everyone had a different tale to report of that heroic night. Thrust and parry, with ships appearing and disappearing with phantasmal unrealism, made it a game of blind man's buff, but buff which spelled death and destruction to more than one man that dreadful night.

The British had the disadvantage of not knowing friend from foe. The Germans knew that any opposition to their break-through must be the British light forces; they guessed by the burning light and the meeting of the 1st British Battle Squadron that Jellicoe's heavy units were steaming south.

More than one bows-on collision occurred during the dark hours. Perhaps the classic one was the British destroyer *Spitfire* which crashed bows on to a German battleship and tore forty feet of her steel plating away. The blast from the German guns tore away her bridge and foremast; the astonishing thing was that she steamed back into harbour, stern first. The authorities at Hull could not understand why she had not immediately sunk. She survived to fight another day.

We admitted to the loss of five destroyers that night: *Tipperary, Turbulent, Ardent, Sparrowhawk* and *Fortune*.

Regarding the *Black Prince*, I visited some years later the French Foreign Legion barracks at Sidi-bel-Abbas in North Africa, from HMS *Delhi* on which I was serving at the time. With a party of five other petty officers we were guests of the *sucre officiers,* a similar military rank to our own. We were there some fourteen hours and they gave us no food at all. We were extremely hungry and eventually went into their mess for a booze up. I did not drink and my companions were not very keen on the 'fire water' these hard-bitten under officers were drinking. They were shouting and dancing on tables, and then my interest was directed to a big German who started a yarn about his brother and the Battle of Jutland. He told me that Hans was in charge of a group of searchlights on one of the battleships.

He told how a British heavy cruiser came out of the midnight dark, large and menacing, all guns and funnels. A cracking order to 'expose beams' commanded them to activity. The white blinding searchlights lanced the darkness and split the night into segments, revealing the ill-fated *Black Prince* already backing away, but it was too late. She was caught by a torrent of bursting shellfire from all calibre of guns. It was carnage; within moments the British cruiser was a mass of twisted metal and, burning like a bush fire, the *Black Prince* was dead in her tracks, a fierce glow in the distant dark, followed by a tremendous catastrophic explosion, lighting up the skies for miles around. Not a man survived.

I did not see any of these actions. Around midnight I went up on deck, up on to the booms of the fore bridge – remember, our 'heads', our lavatories, had been shot away – and away to the north I heard gunfire and saw flashes of orange light against the night sky, and I wondered what was happening out there.

Many years later, as a torpedo instructor I listened to many lectures, and read all the reports issued by both British and German Admiralties on the subject of the Battle of Jutland. At the Torpedo School, HMS Defiance, one episode of the night attack by the 12th Destroyer Flotilla always interested the classes under instruction. It was the most classic encounter of the whole 1914-18 War, and for many years was upheld as an example of the perfect night flotilla attack.

The time back in the steely phosphorescent waters of the Jutland Bank was 1.43 a.m., the wishing hour of the middle watch. So far the 12th Flotilla, led by Captain Sterling, HMS *Faulknor,* and his consorts, *Obedient, Mindful, Marvel, Onslaught, Maenad, Noble, Nerissa* and *Narwhal*, had not been involved in any of the night skirmishes, being well to the east of our main light cruiser advance. For nearly four hours they had been closed up at night defence stations, and goodness knows how many hours before that at day time action stations. Stupefied with fatigue and loss of sleep, eyes red-rimmed, they still stared into the darkness, expecting and hoping to have a go at the enemy. They knew that the light was ideal from the point of view of a torpedo attack.

Suddenly the expected happened: a keen eye spotted a dim silhouette of a line of German battleships appearing darkly out of the shadows, to the west; the 12th Flotilla was obscured by the mist of dawn and the light was such that the burning of searchlights would prove a disadvantage, for the beams would melt into the paleness of the growing light.

This was it! Captain Sterling passed the attack orders down his line of ships by means of a shaded Morse lamp and increased speed to 32 knots. Everything was soon ready – depth, range and speed settings on the torpedoes, safety pins removed from the wicked head pistols. This was to be the attack to be remembered. Everything, both men and weapons, was ready to inflict maximum damage to that line of German warships. On the turn towards them, it could be perceived that there was a considerable number of German enemy ships.

Following their leader, *Faulknor*, every helm went over at the right moment as they arrowed towards the enemy's line – the perfect attack, with an element of surprise, less than a shadow at 3,000 yards, coming out of the dim opaque light. Remembering the losses we had sustained in the daylight action, the grim avengers swept on. Then, as their 'sights' came on, each destroyer fired its torpedoes, and the wicked warheads of 400 lb. of amatol were on their way to death and destruction.

These missiles were scatter fired with the same *élan* as the bowmen at Crecy, but more deadly in their execution.

After firing, each ship turned away into the darkness of the dawn. Jerry spotted the flash from the torpedo tubes 'impulse powder charges' and then all hell was let loose. Every gun that could fire was blazing away but the Germans were still unsure of their targets. They switched on searchlights which only made matters worse as the beams melted into the ghostly blue of the dawning sky and failed to reveal anything. The attacking destroyers, however, now had the glare of the searchlights to aim at, and could watch the enemy's confusion as they swung their ships violently away to avoid the torpedoes.

Torpedo firing officers on each destroyer started their stop watches as they fired, and now waited to see or hear the results of their efforts. Many reported heavy explosions. The crews waited likewise to see any visible effects of their torpedo firing. It seemed to last an eternity and some thought they had missed their targets. Just as the blurred picture of the enemy was fading from their straining eyes, it happened. Suddenly a dull red glow appeared which silhouetted the fore and after parts of an enemy ship. Great flames soared upwards, towering above the two masts of the stricken vessel, and a black domed mushroom of smoke climbed steadily to the skies. Another ship had blown up but this time it was German. It was the pre-Dreadnought battleship *Pommern* and almost 900 men died with her in that fearful nightmare of flaming death.

The flotilla faded away into the darkness except for the *Maenad*. Her Captain, having two torpedoes left in their tubes, decided to attack again. Relying on the element of confusion in the lines of the German ships, the *Maenad* swept in for the kill. Her snaking wake trailed away like the great coils of a boa constrictor, all guns blazing fiercely. Once more the enemy was caught on the wrong foot. The time was just eight minutes after the first attack had ended.

Once again officers and men braced themselves for the supreme moment of death or glory. In came the little destroyer, a ghostly wraith-like figure, with the speed of an albatross, speeding snakelike, with the Quartermaster hanging grimly to a kicking wheel as he fought to answer the Captain's helm orders in the continual alteration of course. The engine room staff responded

DAWN ATTACK BY THE 12th DESTROYER FLOTILLA

1.43 a.m. 1st JUNE 1916

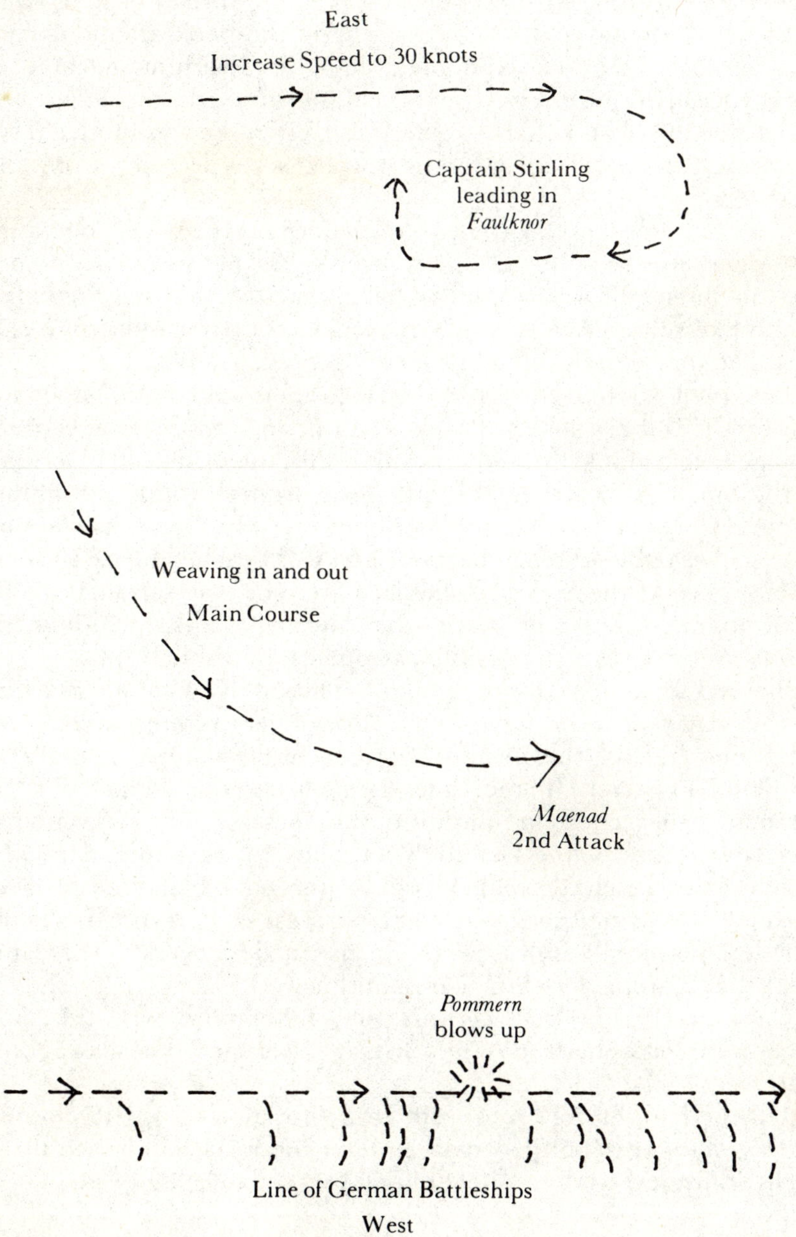

nobly to the call for haste and she exceeded her measured mile speed. In no time the little destroyer was racing in a zig-zag towards the bunched-up lines of German battleships.

The enemy spotted the apparition coming through the opaque light, speeding towards them and threw the book at this daring attacker, every gun that could bear being fired with maniacal fury. A murderous fire from guns of all calibre sprayed the *Maenad* but she seemed to bear a charmed life. More often she was hidden from view by the shell water spouts that enshrouded her from the watchers.

The dull 'flop flop' as the two torpedoes hit the water, one after the other, was seen by the tubes' crews, but not heard as the din was so intense. Over went the helm and the destroyer skidded round like a figure skater, and streaked away on to a safer course. It was then that she was hit and suffered some casualties.

Looking back into the gun-firing hell, they waited and hoped for the result of their daring attack. It came in a short time; a great orange bright flame flushed up from under the bridge of a German battleship. They watched her lurch away from the bunched-up line of panicky ships, but she failed to blow up. The Germans claimed that she was able to reach harbour and was beached in the shallow waters beyond the Sylt Minefields. Later she was salvaged in the same manner as two or three other German ships, including the *Sedlitz, Ostfriesland*, and possibly one other major ship.

Before I leave this episode, I might mention that Captain Sterling of the leader, *Faulknor,* did send out wireless signals to Jellicoe, informing him of the position of the German ships, and of his intention to attack. Three times he sent out this signal, but the Germans succeeded in jamming the message and it was not received in any of the Grand Fleet ships to the south. Had the signals been received, Jellicoe would just have had time to head them off and bring the enemy to action west of the Sylt Minefields. The low-powered wireless sets used in our destroyers at that time were easily jammed and the Germans knew it.

Captain Sterling felt certain that his flotilla was the only organised force between the British Fleet and German home waters.

Jellicoe had, at 9.20 p.m. sent *Abdiel* to lay a minefield close to the Vyl light vessel off Horns Reef after the Fleet had closed up at night. This new, very fast fleet minelayer, capable of a speed of over

40 knots, had been tucked away safely behind Jellicoe's line of battleships during the two short day encounters with the enemy. Her daring foray into German waters paid at least one dividend; the *Ostfriesland*, the German battleship, struck and exploded one of her mines, tearing a great hole in her side. Fortunately for her, the Captain was able to steer her into shallow water and beach her, to be salvaged later.

I often wonder what would have happened if the German Fleet had had to steam the same distance to their home ports that our ships had. I am certain many of their vessels would never have survived that long passage home. We ourselves lost only the heavy cruiser *Warrior,* in spite of the bad weather which blew up during the voyage.

Counting the cost of the night action, our losses were much less than the Germans' in the fierce fighting. We inflicted more punishment in spite of our handicap of being uncertain which was friend and which was foe. This, of course, was due to our night defence disposition. The Germans in their official report admitted the loss of three cruisers: *Elbing, Frauenlob* and *Rostock,* and one battleship, *Pommern.* They also admitted to the loss of one destroyer, the *V-4,* and one torpedoed. Well, reading through all the reports many years later – I wonder! It seemed to me that the Germans concealed a good deal. Destroyers can be built fairly quickly and easily replaced.

Just two more interesting incidents outside of the main skirmishing happened in the early hours of that momentous middle watch.

The survivors of the *Tipperary* had been drifting on a Carley Float through the night from about midnight, when their gallant little craft had been sunk; half frozen with the cold, their lower limbs in water, waiting and hoping to be picked up, straining their eyes in the growing cobwebs of the dawn, they slowly realised that a strange apparition was bearing gradually towards them. They rubbed their salt-encrusted eyes and kept looking, then out of the dawn mist came something that astonished the survivors – a German light cruiser of the Rostock Class appeared like a graveyard ghost. Soundless, deserted, she had no sign of a crew. No one spoke as, with nerves tingling, they waited and watched, then to their astonishment she tilted up her bows and slid backwards, and sank stern first from sight. It happened so slowly, with hardly a ripple left on the water, that it was almost unbelievable.

Later, the exhausted crew of the sinking *Sparrowhawk* had a similar experience. Unable to steam, and only one gun left in action, they drifted through the night, huddled together for warmth round the ship's galley. Silently they waited to be hailed by a friend, dreading to be hailed by a foe. They had fought a grand fight and certainly left their mark on the enemy. The order had been passed that they would not fire their 'pop gun' unless they were forced to. Already a German destroyer had hailed them and, getting no reply, had hurried away into the night.

Slowly out of the morning mist appeared the ghostly form of a battleship or battle cruiser. Gradually the two ships drifted closer and the battered *Sparrowhawk*'s crew could see that she was German. Her guns were pointing upwards, guns of what had been a forrard turret, but were now a mangled mass of broken steel.

It was just light enough to see and say that if anything she was in worse shape than they themselves. Not a man stirred on her decks. She was as quiet as a sepulchre in the monumental deep, a ghost ship. The watchers waited in awe, wondering, then slowly they all perceived that her port list was becoming more pronounced. Then slowly she politely rolled over and with a queer, sighing, gurgling noise she gradually sank from sight, as if reluctant to leave this quiet world of surface peace behind. A sucking vortex set the *Sparrowhawk* rocking like a rowboat on a river, and with a great sigh of relief the crew relaxed. That was the last the world saw of the gallant *Lützow*; she had fought a great battle and this was her last resting place, twelve fathoms deep off the Jutland Bank, to join other sunken wrecks from that great fight.

So the epic night, a night of sinking, burning and torpedoed ships, drew to a close and at 2.30 a.m. on 1st June Jellicoe altered course north and, steaming along the night track, threw out his cruiser screens, hoping to meet and fight the enemy. But it was not to be. Only the pitiful wreckage of that heroic night action met our questing eyes.

Dead men on rafts, floats, lifebuoys, some floating upwards; we even saw some roped together in line, queueing up like citizens waiting for the last tram long since gone by, pitiful flotsam, the aftermath of war was all that was to be seen. There was no enemy ship in sight apart from a solitary Zeppelin. Many ships unloaded their guns on to this target including *Tiger*, but the airship disdainfully tilted its nose and flew slowly up into the skies, at the same time reporting the presence of the British Fleet.

Jellicoe and Beatty searched the seas. Then a signal from British Admiralty told the story that the German High Seas Fleet had escaped home and were now safe behind their own minefields. Through the low cloud wrack and morning mist came the outpost cruisers and destroyers, all reporting nothing but the pitiful few survivors and action wreckage. So Jellicoe dispersed from action stations.

Now let us return to the point when the *Tiger* went to night defence stations, after we had fired our last daylight rounds of angry gunfire.

Just after 9 p.m. we went to our night disposition, in our case of course remaining closed up at our guns. We now managed to have a meal. I well remember seeing our august paymaster, coat off, sleeves rolled up, knee deep in loaves of bread and cans of corned beef, making sandwiches for the troops, surrounded by a motley crowd of 'dry idlers', writers, storekeepers and cooks.

I went up on the booms to pump ship and looked around. All was fairly quiet. The ship was just cruising along at roughly 18 to 20 knots, keeping formation with the remainder of the Grand Fleet. We knew of no portent of what the future held for us, we had only to inherit the decease of human events.

While eating our meal, one of our RNVR messmates staggered into the gun casement and I shall never forget the look on that poor lad's face. Racked with pain and covered in blood, his left arm was splintered and pock-marked by shell fragments. He stood swaying on his feet with exhaustion and one of our boys caught him before he fell, easing him down on to the hatch of the ammunition hoist. He had been the rangetaker of Q turret which had received that nasty wallop from one of Jerry's '11'.

We gave him a drink of cocoa and, in spite of his protests that other poor lads required the doctor's attentions more urgently, two of us took him down to the casualty clearing station. Half an hour later, feeling and looking much better, he returned to us for food, his arm in a sling and his tattered clothes removed, wearing a stoker's dungaree coat.

Protesting that he must return to Q turret, he took some sandwiches and left. We did not have the heart to quench his gallant spirit by retaining him. During the night reports kept coming in to both flagships, ours and the enemy's, on the state of the Fleets for action.

In spite of losing so far more ships, we were very much better off as regards damage and readiness for immediate, impending action. Our Battle Fleet had all guns fit for firing, and this included the *Marlborough* and the *Warspite,* despite torpedo damage to the former and some damage by gunfire to *Warspite.* The battle cruisers, handicapped by the loss of three ships – *Indefatigable, Queen Mary* and *Invincible* – were still vastly superior in numbers and guns fit to fire. But in the case of the enemy, Jellicoe knew that their battle cruisers were no longer a fighting force. Our light cruisers had reported this fact.

With *Lützow* sinking or sunk, *Seydlitz*'s forecastle and upper deck lapping the water's edge, guns unable to fire, *Derfflinger* in a similar position, *Von Der Tann* only a ghost of her former self, this left *Moltke* in almost as bad a condition, trying her utmost to shepherd the halt and the lame home to shallow waters or to be beached. As for the German Battle Fleet, the terrible weight of British gunfire in the two encounters had left their mark on the once proud and much vaunted German High Seas Fleet.

Consequently, later that night Jellicoe despatched both *Warspite* and *Marlborough* to make their way back home for dockyard repairs.

However, to return once more to the time under discussion. We settled down around our guns for the night and waited, smoking, dozing and listening. As mentioned previously, I went up on to the booms around midnight and heard gunfire to the north, but felt too exhausted to take a great deal of notice of the sound.

After the disappointment of the morning action stations, at 2.30 a.m. on 1st June we gave up our spare hammocks to the Bosun for sewing up our dead for burial, and then I proceeded alone on a tour of the ship. My first place of call was the Medical Distribution space. I had heard that my friend, Teddie Brown, had been wounded.

I found the place forrard to the right of B turret barbette, and overflowing on to the starboard stokers' mess deck. Brown was doing fairly well so I moved among my wounded shipmates. What a scene it was! It was very much like that painting of the *Victory*'s cockpit, ill lit, with mutilated bodies lying everywhere. The few cots were full, all hammock places occupied. The remainder were lying on mess tables and on the hard steel lino-covered decks, pitiful wrecks of this terrible action.

I stopped by the hammock of a seaman acquaintance of mine, lit a cigarette and put it between his lips. He had lost both arms but seemed remarkably cheerful that the *Tiger* had done so well in the action. That brave man's cheerfulness made me think that the human spirit was certainly not a candle in the storm of time.

Away in one corner, close to the ship side, I could hear a seaman reciting the Twenty-third Psalm, 'The Lord is My Shepherd, I shall Not Want', and thought that someone was about to quit this world. I felt very sad and turned away, leaving this scene of desolation, soul-destroying wreckage of humanity. I left the wounded to the care of their ministering male angels and as I mounted the ladder, the burnt cases, hooded faces in their picric acid bandages, eyes slit, seemed to follow me.

I learned later from one of the sick berth attendants, a friend of mine, that during the height of the action a very badly wounded stoker came stumbling into the fore distributing station, and over the doorway combing dropped what had been a human form, a trunk with no arms and legs, and saying to the fleet surgeon who bent over him, 'See if you can dish Shortie up, please, sir. He is in a bad way.' The whispered voice sank away, with the body, to the bloodstained deck. 'Greater love hath no man ...'

I walked forrard through the great armoured doorway, wheel operated by hand, at least four inches of good British steel. The Sick Bay flat was a shambles – glass, wood, and steel strewn everywhere, and the nauseating smell of chemicals thick in the air. To the left of it had once been the Chief Petty Officers' Mess but now the bulkhead and deck was one gaping hole, with dark satanic water sloshing about. It made me shudder. I looked up and forrard, saying to myself that it was no place for me. I could smell chlorine gas escaping from the battery room above the fore submerged torpedo flat. Great glass carboys of acid had been smashed by the exploding shell and, despite the thick lead flooring, had eaten into the doorway lintel and started to mix with the sea water in the fore capstan flat. The submerged torpedo crew had escaped death because of the armoured decking and hatch. They had climbed to safety by means of the torpedo hatchway, up on to the forecastle.

I retreated aft and up a hatchway outside the ship galley, and along the deck forrard. The whole of our anchoring equipment had been destroyed except the one anchor and cable on the starboard side. The capstan and port cable holder had been demolished.

Returning aft along the after forecastle deck on the starboard side, were laid out a number of gas wounded, a dreadful sight, grey-green in appearance. These men had probably suffered more than any others wounded in the action. A friend of mine, Paddy Doyle, had died in this manner.

Then I came upon a graveyard of desolation. On the port side the sailmaker and his mates were preparing the victims of this sad action for burial, and the sweet, sickly smell of death still lingers now in my memory. I shall always remember that meeting with the dead, some of whom were shattered beyond any semblance of human form.

I inspected Q turret again and could understand how lucky we had been in being able to fire one gun after the gun house had received the full force of such an explosion. The after forecastle upper deck had been ripped by shellfire but not enough to worry about. X turret had withstood the shell explosion very well on the after side of the great steel barbette.

I went down the after hatchway and had a look at what I considered the worst hit place of the whole action, the after port ammunition passage. Here were two feet of salt water, phosphorescent in the ghostly glow from dim emergency lighting strung overhead. The port 6 inch magazine had had to be flooded to save the ship from blowing up. A fire had raged here, a fragment of the shell having damaged the port engine room, but not seriously although it had been filled with smoke. The fire and repair party, and ammunition supply party, had all been killed or wounded, our heaviest casualties. The cruel slivers of hot steel cut into flesh and bone of the men gathered there, and the blast of the explosion had gathered up the bodies and dashed them against the steel bulkheads to fall like broken dolls, silent and still in the dark satantic waters sloshing through the shell hole of the shattered ship side. The six inch gun hoist had been wrecked beyond repair. The armature of the electric motor was sticking into the centre of the winch operator. A single 12 inch shell had done this entire damage.

I went forrard through the port 6 inch battery, then down the port forrard hatchway to the port stokers' messdeck. Here was more trouble. A heavy German shell had exploded against B turret barbette protecting the magazine. The main force of the explosion had been taken up by the shell penetrating the ship's side and partly exploding in the flour store. What a mess that was! Salt water and Canadian flour – the place was like a huge 'duff', one sticky and glutinous mass. The chief trouble here was that the crew of the low-powered electric generating room had been trapped beneath the flour store.

The pumps were dealing with the water but the hatch had become buckled and slowly water was seeping down into the generating room below. Everyone feared that eventually the water would rise to the level of the 20-volt generators and so put out of action the low-powered systems. If that happened, the secondary batteries would last for only a few hours and power would then fail to the gun control circuits, searchlights and torpedo circuits, telephone exchanges and the 20-volt lighting systems in various parts of the ship. Navigation instruments, including the gyro compass and its repeaters, would also be affected.

Our Captain up on the bridge kept up a word of good cheer, telephoning every quarter of an hour to the trapped lower power crew, promising them release as soon as possible. Many hours later by means of crowbars and chain purchases, the armoured hatch was forced open sufficiently to allow escape for the courageous crew. The leading wireman received the DCM for his part in this episode.

That evening, after a rough clean up of the ship, we went on deck to the Burial Service. The time was then about 7 p.m. We had seen it all before at the Dogger Bank action but this time we had to bury a large number of our dead shipmates.

The ship, losing speed, just glided through the water with a gentle, lulling flop, flop of the sea wavelets hitting the steel of the ship's sides. The remains of our shipmates lying on deal planks with a 100 lb shot at their feet were wrapped in the Union Jack. Then the service began, the sonorous voice of our Padre breaking in on our thoughts and silent prayers, and our tears became the salt of sadness.

The 'Last Post' was sounded by the massed buglers, poignantly clear in the quiet air, as the pallbearers lifted each plank, one by one, and then in unison the bodies released hit the water. The lifting notes of the bugle call 'Reveille' and then the quiet order 'Dismiss' followed. There is nothing quite so moving as the burial of a shipmate at sea.

Now came the time to count the cost. As a ship we could still steam at full speed and we could fire all our guns except the right gun of Q. We had received, we discovered later, twenty-one hits, two 12 inch, fourteen 11 inch, and five 5.9 inch shells, and the amount of rounds of ammunition we had fired were 304 13.5 inch and 140 6 inch shells and one torpedo.

There was no doubt – to be able to live and fight in *Tiger* again, she would have to be repaired by the dockyard.

Now we had the real job of clearing up the mess. Our ship in many places reminded one of a municipal dustbin, a refuse heap of one-time normality. Before that happened, however, we had to account for the missing. The Roll was called and the Seamen and Royal Marines, RMLI and RMA, were found correct. However, of the stokers some were found but some were never located and were put down to have been Killed in Action. It had not been possible to identify many of the remains. The 'off watch' stokers had formed the main action repair and fire parties and had therefore been in the thick of the action, receiving the heaviest casualties.

To return for a moment to the action. I did not realise that our giant-looking mastodon, the main range-finder, the Argo Tower, had received a very severe hit early in the 'Run to the South'. A hit in the base of it had lifted the huge armoured bulk off its mounting but eventually it rocked back into place again. This high-powered shell caused some damage and loss of life.

About four days later, we found the stoker belonging to the engineer captain's steam pinnace. This character was known as 'Steamboat Bill' and was admired and regarded most affectionately by everyone. He was a man with an outstanding personality. He was found by a searching shipmate in the wreckage of the port ammunition passage. The jammed door had been freed and there was Steamboat, with the usual half-grin he wore on his pleasant face, standing upright behind it, bolt upright like a waxwork figure at Madame Tussaud's, very lifelike, but very dead. He had qualified for citizenship of the grave. The searcher had been so sure that he would be found alive that he spoke to Steamboat, but alas Steamboat had been killed by the concussion of the shell explosion. The port 6 inch ammunition passage gave up two more dead men that day.

By this time an awful smell had penetrated all over the ship and we had to get busy with buckets of disinfectant and carbolic soap.

Human flesh had got into all sorts of nooks, such as voice pipes, telephones, ventilating shafts and behind bulkheads. I remember helping to clear the port flour store of that glutinous mass of water and flour; it was like trying to clear out a huge pastry-mixing bowl, and we humans were the currants! What a mess it was!

However, returning for a moment to a couple of days previously. We arrived steaming into harbour, and going under the Forth Bridge our soldier friends asked us a question that was full of emotion for us, 'Where's the *Queen Mary*?' No one had the heart to answer. We could not moor our ship, only use the starboard anchor, so we tied up alongside the dockyard at Rosyth.

Once again Sir David Beatty spoke to us, the whole of the Battle Cruiser Fleet, every man jack except the fire party. We all assembled on the north side of the dockyard wall. I can hear his voice now, clear and resonant: 'Well, boys, we have won a great victory and I am sorry with you that we were not able to finish the job and sink the lot.' That was the gist of his speech and he went on to say he hoped one day we should have another chance.

I well remember the visit of our former First Lord of the Admiralty, Prince Louis of Battenberg, during our spell in dock. I was with a party of seamen about to clean out the flour store when Captain Pelly was taking Sir David Beatty and Prince Louis around the ship, and pointing out how well *Tiger* had stood up to the enemy's shellfire. They had reached B turret barbette and Pelly was commenting on the toughness of the armour belt. The explosion had only caused a dent in the steel.

We stood to attention and Prince Louis noticed us and came and spoke, saying, 'Well done, boys, you and your ship did very well and I am proud of you all.' We stammered our thanks and he smiled and rejoined Sir David and Captain Pelly. We thought that was praise indeed coming from such a distinguished officer.

We now knew the extent of our losses and I will quote a few statistics:

*Number of ships of both Fleets at Jutland.*

| *British* (Dreadnoughts) | *German* |
|---|---|
| 28 Battleships | 16 Dreadnought Battleships |
| 9 Battle Cruisers | 6 pre-Dreadnoughts |
| 33 Cruisers, all types | 5 Battle Cruisers |

(Continued)

| *British* | *German* |
|---|---|
| 1 Seaplane Carrier | 11 Cruisers |
| 1 Minelayer | 71 Destroyers |
| 80 Destroyers | |

*Losses*

| | |
|---|---|
| 3 Battle Cruisers | 1 old Battleship |
| 3 Cruisers | 1 Battle Cruiser |
| 8 Destroyers | 4 Cruisers |
| | 5 Destroyers |

The German battle cruisers took ten months to be repaired.

These are the numbers admitted by both antagonists.

However, the main fact was that we had won a great moral and tactical victory, and this was freely admitted later by many experts. The German Admiralty was determined never to allow their ships to face the terrible might of the British Fleet in open battle again.

*British Casualties:* 364 Officers and 6,324 Men were killed and wounded.

One thing we did learn later by means of our information system was that the Germans put canvas screens around their ships to prevent civilians learning the extent of the damage to their much vaunted Fleet.

Whole upper works swept clean overboard on many of their major ships and great piles of dead littered the wharfs; scores of ambulances left the dockyard carrying the wounded to hospitals. I do not believe that we did anything to try to hide the extent of our damage or casualties.

It was a considerable time before the German ships were repaired, but in the case of the British Fleet, the Admiralty were informed by Jellicoe that the whole of the British Grand Fleet, less the two battleships *Marlborough* and *Warspite,* whose place in the line had been taken by one ship in dockyard hands at the time of Jutland, HMS *Queen Elizabeth,* eight 15 inch guns, and HMS *Resolution* (just completing her battle training, a newly commissioned ship after her dockyard trials had been completed, an 'R' class battleship, with eight 15 inch guns) were now ready to put to sea. Sir David Beatty also reported four battle cruisers were now ready for sea after re-fuelling, and HMS *Australia* was now action fit after her collision with *New Zealand* during the middle of May.

The dockyard repairs took us three weeks to complete, which meant that our crew had a week's leave to each watch, two watches going on leave together. Well do I remember that leave and home-coming, proudly wearing the name cap ribbon: HMS TIGER.

Never shall I forget that happy time all the way down from Rosyth; we were feted like royalty. At Preston the dear ladies opened the carriage doors and I remember amidst the black acrid smoke from the belching engine a voice from a kinder world saying, 'Tea and cakes, gentlemen,' in such sweet tones. The gruff deep water men were greatly moved by their kindness. I looked out of the carriage door, it was a wet and stormy scene and the lightning sprang out of the night sky like a glittering leaf. The time must have been about two bells in the middle watch then anon, and as the 'Grand Fleet Special' roared through the night our hearts were lifted in spite of ignorant criticism from the ill-informed Press that our hard fought action at Jutland had been a defeat for the British battle cruisers. The night before, we bought evening papers at Edinburgh's Waverley Station and read the King's message of the truth at Jutland, and also comments favourable from the American Press that Von Scheer had turned tail and bolted for home and safety; also the true comments of our late First Lord of the Admiralty, Jackie Fisher's praise for Jellicoe's masterly handling of the mighty British Fleet and his telling comment: 'A great tactical and moral victory for the Royal Navy.' He also stressed that Sir David Beatty had with great honour and skilled handling of his battle cruisers, in spite of a loss of a third of his force, fulfilled his duty of leading the Germans on the rapacious guns of Jellicoe's magnificent Battle Fleet.

Yes, seven days' glorious leave! A real rest from the heartbreak of war. We were walking on air and terribly thrilled after the sneers of some of the dockyard men in Rosyth Dockyard. Some even booed us when we arrived alongside the wall, weary and shell-shocked. Millions of people had been misled by the badly written report from the British Admiralty and the stupid boasting from the rhetoric of the senior German naval officers and reported by Reuter's correspondent. At Birmingham Station New Street, the telegraphed relatives were anxiously searching for loved ones like Customs Officers looking for the contraband of war.

To us, our success was very much like the Elixir of Youth! We felt on the crest of the wave, full of happiness. All we had hoped and trained for had come true – 'To the Victor the Spoils.'

On leave in Cheltenham I watched dozens of people nudge one another when seeing me, and many others came up to say, 'Excuse me, Jack, may I touch your collar for luck?' They seemed to regard the three rows of tape superimposed on the blue jean as the Midas touchstone. Many others shook my hand, many elderly ladies and fair young maidens kissed me heartily, saying, 'God bless you, Jack.' I felt I was walking on air. In the local, I was never allowed to pay for a drink.

Soon we were all back on board. Then unfortunately we ran into trouble. The dockyard workmen annoyed us at night when we wished to sleep by using their pneumatic drills and 'windy' hammers. No doubt they were only acting under orders but the loss of sleep and the continual din at night was immensely irritating. Eventually we succeeded in obtaining a distribution of sleeping billets.

Anyhow, we were soon out of dock and back at sea again with our Squadron. Sir David Beatty was glad to take his boys back into German waters for a 'shake up' cruise.

## CHAPTER 8

# Beatty Sweeps the Kattegat and the Steel Monsters Prey for the Last Time

In August we thought for a fleeting moment that we were going to have another Jutland – same place and shallow water, with good weather. It was a forlorn hope and stillborn. A Zeppelin spotted our light forces, led by Admiral Tyrwhitt, and turned sixteen points to scuttle off home again.

The Germans did poke their noses out of harbour but only just; very soon they scampered back again. Their depleted Fleet was hopelessly outmatched by our extra ships which had recently come into commission to join the Fleet. Jackie Fisher's 'Phantoms' were already joining, or getting ready to join, the Fleet and *Courageous* and *Glorious* proved unsuitable as battle cruisers, and were converted into aircraft carriers. *Repulse* and *Renown* very light but very fast, hard-hitting battle cruisers would soon be a powerful addition to the Fleet.

I remember that it was a very good summer in the North Sea in 1916 and I watched many an ethereal dawn breaking through the early morning mists, a faint gossamer light growing brighter every moment until the golden ball of the rising sun would tip above the horizon. Leaning on the guard rails, smoking quietly, a whole line of sailors would watch and marvel at the wonders of the deep.

Most ships of the Fleet were by now weirdly and wonderfully camouflaged. Dazzle colours, false bow waves and stern wash – at times you could hardly tell whether they were coming or going. I well remember the old *Inflexible*; her paint was ancient having been first used for the Dardanelles campaign; she had a brazen appearance like that of a wandering harlot in a polka dot dress.

We were often at sea but not with any high hopes of bringing the enemy to decisive action. I remember on one occasion that Jerry had a submarine net laid out which actually worked, and they bagged the *Nottingham* and *Lowestoft* light cruisers. These German submarines did well but we were not without our slice of luck, because we in our turn torpedoed the German battleship SMS *Thüringen* just inside the enemy coastline, as the Germans retreated in alarm behind their own minefields and the safety of shallow waters.

I saw the cruiser *Nottingham* sink. She went down gradually by the bow, getting lower in the water and her stern rising inch by inch, then suddenly she seemed to arrow down into the depths below quickly, as if to say, 'Let's get it over.' Her crew had already been taken off by a destroyer.

All this happened when Jellicoe and Beatty were on one of their periodical sweeps with the knowledge that the Germans might come out of port. But the Germans were only toying with the idea, and it was good propaganda for the failing morale of their people.

Walking through the dockyard at Rosyth one summer evening, after playing water polo at Dunfermline, I spoke to a dockyard bobby. He told me of the arrest of Carl Loder, the famous German spy. He had been captured by a zealous policeman who had noticed that Loder was in the same place at the same time for two or three days, and that he was always on the same viaduct. When questioned, the policeman observed that the man's command of English seemed particularly pronounced. Loder was subsequently shot in the Tower of London.

We led a sort of tight life, rather tense all the while. At sea or in harbour there were so many dangers to the ships of the Fleet, from U-boat torpedoes to enemy mines laid from surface craft, but more often laid by large minelaying submarines. The danger of aerial attack was always with us from Zeppelins. All this was in addition to the usual hazards of navigation at sea caused by fog and steaming at night with no navigation lights, showing only a glimmer from a shaded stern light of low candle power. And our greatest consolation was of course letters from home. Postage was without payment for all active service fighting men.

At sea, very little letter writing was done, at least by the seamen, being messed in the 6 inch gun casement. Our tables and stools were triced up overhead so that the guns could be brought into immediate action. We ate our meals sitting on upturned buckets and gun and mess tubs, putting our plates, etc. on the deck.

In harbour, after coaling ship, was a real get-together; most sailors after supper having their ditty boxes open on the mess tables would be writing letters to their loved ones. Inside each box lid would be a picture gallery of mums and dads, brothers and sisters, wives and sweethearts, or the latest 'piece of fluff'. The few married men would proudly exclaim, 'Look at my nipper! I made him that suit of navy blue.' If you were not writing, you would walk around and admire these picture galleries and hear the latest home gossip.

Shipmates are the friendliest people in the world and will stick by one another through storm and fine weather, and very honest they are. In my day one could leave a month's 'compo' (pay) on the mess table and no one would steal it. It just was not done. They might borrow your clothes when in a fix but not steal your money.

If a man died, his kit was put up for auction and sold, and resold, for fantastic sums of money, to send home to his dependants.

It was about October 1916, that the event occurred which came to be known as the 'Great Discovery'.

Every month, without fail, Chief Stoker Kelly, DCM, etc. etc. etc. and so forth – he had only one medal less than the King, so rumour had it – and his wing coal bunker party would inspect the dark black diamond containers, huge cavities at the side of the ship. They were spaced around next to the armour belt and one of the reasons for this particular position was to act as an extra armour for the ship's side, besides being emergency fuel storages.

'Darby' Kelly and his henchmen were ventilating these wing bunkers one day. His stokers were down in one of these great coal cellars situated in one corner of our gun casement, close to my mess. I was having a basin of tea – no cups and saucers in the Navy of those days – when a shout of glee and a blackened face appeared above the rim of the bunker, calling, 'Eureka! I have found it!' Darby almost ran to meet him and then a hurried consultation took place. Finally the great Chief Stoker Kelly went down into the bunker shaft like a disappearing diver descending. As he went I heard him saying, 'Oh, me bhoy, oh, me bhoy,' with immense glee, and I wondered what it was all about.

A little later up came a grinning stoker, asking me for a rope's end and I passed down the ammunition hoist rope, then watched two exhilarated stokers and the dour-looking Darby Kelly hauling up a very battered wall safe. Suddenly the 'penny dropped' and I remembered that the safe had been one which stood against the bulkhead, on a shelf in the dry goods canteen, in the covered-in starboard after forecastle deck. I also recollected some talk about it after the action, how it could not be found and so on, and eventually it was logged as blown overboard in action. Of course, everyone was upset because, I believe, the insurance company had already paid out to 'Millars Canteens Ltd.'

Apparently the stokers' fire party had swiped the safe and tried every trick they could think of to open it – crowbars, coal hammers, coal slices and so on, but to no avail. Finally they had decided to hide it in the wing bunker. The story, of course, went right round the Fleet and was regarded as a huge joke for some time.

Slowly the summer burnt itself out, then suddenly the face of winter was once again showing itself, blowing its cruel way across the waters of the North Sea.

Finally 1916 died without many further incidents worth mentioning, and on the last day of the Old Year we went into Rosyth Dockyard. We had fitted a dozen armoured plates around our ship's side and 2 inch armoured upper deck plates around the turrets, to explode enemy shells, to protect our heavy gun magazines; this was one of the lessons learned at the Jutland action.

I did not go on leave with the main party but was detailed for the duties of Ship's Police. This was rather an eerie job at night, with the ship deathly quiet and only a few men on board. We were unarmed apart from a stick which was not much more than an overgrown cane. We wore rubber-soled shoes so that we could go everywhere in the ship. The cordite magazines were empty but the shell rooms still had their complement of live shells.

I was often startled by a squealing black rat and frequently longed for company as I walked around, shining my torch into dark places. We had to look out for spies and saboteurs, several of our ships having been blown up in suspicious circumstances. We did catch a party of workmen in the Wireless Silent Cabinet which was marked Secret and arrested them, turning them over to the dockyard police. Later I enquired about them and a policeman told me that they would be shot in the Tower if they turned out to be spies. However, if they were only skulking they would be sent out in the army to the Western Front. He remarked, 'Looks as if they will be shot in any case, mate.'

It was during this period that John Brown, the builder of *Tiger* at Clydebank, Scotland, entertained our ship's company to a dinner and dance. He was so proud of our now very famous battle cruiser;

Fleet Street called us 'one of Beatty's beautiful cats'. The ladies present were the wives or daughters of the men who had helped to build the ship. It was a great time although I was unable to be present, being home on leave.

After a very refreshing leave I found myself with my shipmates back at sea again.

About this time I remember another incident. It was the day that MacVitie, one of our gun crew RNVRs from the Clyde Division had a heart attack. Rear Admiral R.Y. Tyrwhitt, DSO, commanding the Harwich Force in HMS *Centaur,* was out at sea taking part in a second attack on the Zeppelin Sheds at Cuxhaven, by means of sea planes lowered over the side from converted merchantmen. They flew off from the quiet waters of the Heligoland Bight.

We in the battle cruisers did not actually take any active part in this action, remaining well out of sight in the North Sea to the south-west of Jutland Bank, we were not closed up for action but were on watch at SI 6 inch gun. MacVitie and I were standing just outside the casement on the upper deck when a Zeppelin put in an appearance and, without warning, B turret opened up with 13.5 inch shrapnel. The gun blast caught us both and we were whirled along the upper deck like leaves before a storm. I caught Mac by the collar with my left hand, and we lay gasping. My chum was deathly white. I carried him eventually into the gun casement where we sent for the Fleet Surgeon. His heart had been affected and he was removed to hospital; we did not see him again.

Even with the loss of three battle cruisers we managed to maintain three squadrons of battle cruisers, the 1st Squadron, *Lion,* fleet flagship, *Princess Royal* flag, *Tiger.* The 2nd Squadron: *New Zealand,* flag, *Australia.* The 3rd Squadron: *Indomitable,* flag, with *Inflexible.*

We knew that we should soon have replacements; new ships were about to join our squadrons.

The year 1917 came and we were still always at sea, hoping to meet the enemy, but somehow we felt that our hour had passed and that Jerry would only meet us again in perhaps a hit-and-run encounter, rather than in open warfare.

We now came to the grimmest part of the whole war. The U-boat warfare had reached its peak of successful intensity, leaving great gaps in our merchant fleet which could not be filled. We were getting desperately short of food, not far short of famine.

Jellicoe left the Grand Fleet to take over as First Lord of the Admiralty. He found out that chance ideas were being flung freely, but never from the bow of logic and soon he and his staff decided to try out the old idea used in the days of commerce raiding by 'ships of the line' in the age old sailing navies of the maritime nations and use the convoy system, which soon proved successful. Beatty took over Jellicoe's job of Commander-in-Chief of the Grand Fleet. At Rosyth, Vice-Admiral Phillimore, whom we have previously spoken about, the Captain of the gallant *Warspite,* was now in charge of the battle cruiser force. He flew his flag in HMS *Repulse*, the new fast but lightly-armoured battle cruiser.

I must tell you how we fared in the Fleet as regards food. First of all, the staff of life, a $2\frac{1}{2}$lb. loaf was shared between three men for a period of 24 hours. Regarding meat, in the eighteenth century that great diarist and controller of the Navy, Samuel Pepys, carried out a series of food reforms for victualling the fleet. The most important of these orders was the salting down of vast quantities of pork, and storing them at Deptford Navy Yard, using what was then known as 100lb. casks. Well, his successors carried out this reform, so that when 1914 came there was a vast store of salt pork all ready to feed Britain's huge fleet for many weeks. The casks were burnt marked with a red hot stamping iron with the words '1802', '1803', etc. (shades of Nelson!), a broad naval arrow, and 'Deptford'. And when the fully released fury of the U-boat campaign broke upon us, this store of food was a godsend to the Fleet in home waters.

I can see our ship's cooks now, knocking the hoops off the casks and 'shaking' the staves, then tying heaving lines around the salt pork, which was as hard as iron, and securing one end of the rope lines to throw the pork lumps over the ship side at sea, and tow the meat for twenty-four hours to soak away the salt. After that, to soak in Cookie's great copper for a further long period in warm, fresh water, and then boiling in the same copper for four hours, with split peas and lentils – a meal fit for a king!

At one time there was only horseflesh, and very stringy animals they proved, too. My advice to anyone about to eat horseflesh is – don't! It has a sweetish, lingering taste that I found I could not bear, rather like eating Dead Sea fruit. We even tried eating seagulls, catching them with fishing line, but their flavour was little better.

Then someone had a brainwave; we set to and all the ship's

company made seining nets to catch fish. This was a great success for a time, until jack sprat got wise to us and all of a sudden the harbours seemed empty. However, we succeeded in persuading the fleet drifters to go out to sea to catch some for us.

Meanwhile, the back room boys had been busy, and with the new type of depth charge, and the forerunner of the Asdic listening device as well, more and more escorts became available to help with the convoy work. The food situation improved slightly and we no longer found it necessary to lock our bread ration away, to prevent it being stolen, an idea which was entirely foreign to us.

Then, just before the Americans entered the war, they escorted part of the convoys some of the way from America.

Up at Scapa, Beatty got the merchant ship *Gourka* converted into a concert ship, the bulkheads being removed; this was a great success as a whole ship's company could enjoy a concert at once. Then we were granted recreation leave, the first time for two whole years; we could play games and drink munition beer in a wet canteen; admittedly it was very much under-proof beer, but it had 'any port in a storm' sort of idea. It was a little better than the onion beer that was sold at one time during the war in pubs here; its origins were a mystery to everyone.

All the Boys 1st Class were now of the age to be rated Ordinary or Able Seamen; in nearly every case they were rated ABs and of course messed with the seamen, and now we really had to learn all about canteen messing and not be spoon fed by the Paymasters' General messing system, in which the ship's cooks did all the work. In canteen messing, the Paymaster supplied most of the food in bulk, such as bread and flour, meat and vegetables, tea, sugar and tinned milk, corned beef and salmon, all condiments, slabs of rich fat streaked cocoa, and by the way, it is quite true that it is not properly made unless the large spoon stands bolt upright at attention unaided in the mess fanny. And if you sleep, say in the morning watch after the middle, drinking lashings of this viscuous delightful beverage, you will dream hallucinations phantasmal! – in other words, get 'cocoa rats'. Also we were issued with plum and apricot jam.

Well, our midday dinner was prepared by the two duty cooks of the mess detailed on a rota system by the leading rating. We learnt from the old hands how to make a meat pie, 'Tiddy Oggies', toad in the hole, 'Open air pie with no awning', and if you were a bad cook or pushed for time, it would be a 'straight rush' nicknamed 'Hello Butch Hello Cookie'. This would be the spuds peeled and the meat slapped on top. For tea it would be tea and bread and marg, and if it was someone's birthday someone would try and make a cake, but 'Slushy' (name for ship's cooks) would send it back in the form of a duff, often wet and soggy. Our galley was a good oil-fired affair, but with over a thousand hands to cook for – well, I ask you!

For breakfast and dinner all the cooks operated, but for cooked suppers, the duty cook watched the matelots at work.

The Paymaster allowed each rating 4½d. per day messing allowance, and each mess was allowed extra food from the 'Pusser' if required. All mess food including canteen grocery was paid for by a chit system. Individual food from the 'can waller' canteen was a cash payment. On the first of each month it would be a mess bill, but if your mess caterer was careful, it could be a Paymaster's rebate.

Later in the year I went on leave and was immediately struck by the absence of men; all Britain's manpower seemed to be on the Western Front. In Cheltenham, a few elderly policemen, old men and some wounded soldiers appeared to be the only men about. There were a great many young servant girls and shop assistants pushing wounded soldiers in bath chairs. All the large empty houses had been turned into hospitals and many of the parks had been ploughed up to provide food. This was still in very short supply; many people had an almost starved look about them. It seemed to everyone that England stood with her back to the wall; however, the 'Welsh Wizard' was now Prime Minister – Lloyd George – and we could at last see the silver lining.

Then the Navy went over from defence to the attack in U-boat warfare, and many German submarines met their doom. Their monthly lists of sunken vessels grew and Grand Admiral Tirpitz became greatly perturbed. The days of easy pickings were over.

With the depth charge soon came the 'Thrower', a type of gun which could throw a 500lb. of TNT or Amatol fifty to one hundred yards, to help in the attack. Also our improved mine barriers in the English Channel and North Sea, like mature trees, began to bear fruit and many a U-boat was blown up and destroyed by the new British horned mines.

Gradually the merchant sinkings became less and less each month. Fast ships of 16 knots and over were unescorted, and routed on unusual courses to their destinations, while at home munitions factories were now pouring out the tools of war.

Then it came like a light from heaven – the entry of America at last into the War on our side. This caused a tremendous sensation. I can still recall these great battleships of theirs with their curious trellis masts, and with names that rolled off one's tongue with the lilt of an Irving Berlin melody – *Texas, Tennessee, Wyoming, Maryland,* and so on.

We in the British Fleet taught them the art of fast coaling and Admiral Sims was most grateful to us. I remember seeing the whole Allied Fleet at sea on exercise, a tremendous sight of naval power, over forty battleships and nearly two hundred light craft.

On 21st November 1917, the big guns spoke for the last time. Beatty was once more sweeping the Kattegat, that narrow neck of land-locked waters leading into Germany and the Baltic. We had carried out this manoeuvre dozens of times and knew what to expect and how to carry it out. Using our light forces as bait, we swept in. Alexander Sinclair, in his new flagship *Cardiff,* one of the famous C class of cruisers, led the way. Into the confined waters steamed our outposts. The weather was fine, without much actual sun, very high light cloud and very good visibility.

Our light forces' daring foray was a dangerous one; there was not a great deal of room to make a leeway from the point of view of action. They had to face their last enemy – their own fears. There were no story book heroics here. Nervously alert, they steamed into what could be a trap, for we knew that Jerry had left harbour; if he was in these waters it could be very much a do or die effort. We in the battle cruisers, led by Admiral Phillimore, were not far away, that is, the 1st Battle Cruiser Squadron *Repulse,* leading *Lion, Princess Royal,* flagship of Sir Walter Cowan, *Tiger*.

Suddenly *Cardiff*'s masthead man began to report smoke to the south-east, then heavy smoke began to smudge the horizon. It was apparently coming from ships which lay just out of sight, and Sinclair began to report.

Soon the masthead man and then the spotting top and director personnel began to report the top hamper of ships, and it was obvious that the enemy was in sight.

We in the battle cruisers were already at action stations. I was still serving S.3 6 inch guns, although I had been promoted to able seaman torpedo-man, which should have given me a torpedo or electrical actions station; however, the order was still in force: stay at one's trained position for warfare. I was able, therefore, to get once again a bird's eye view through the eyes of our friend up in the 6 inch gun control tower. This voice pipe commentator started off well: 'Heavy smoke to the south-east, boys.' Then, a little later, 'Increasing speed. *Repulse* going like a bomb. Got a bone in her gizzard! We are off now! Good Alf Bentick is giving her the big stick.' His remarks were quite humorous at times.

We felt that this was it! We were not prepared to go too far in so the encounter might well be short and sharp. It would be too risky to proceed beyond a certain limit, because German minefields could be waiting to trap us.

We waited, but not for long. A low rumble like distant thunder echoed across the waters, indicating enemy gunfire from a long way off, then the sharper notes of lower calibre guns could be heard nearer to us. We could guess that the 1st Light Cruiser Squadron was in action. Then with the violence of velocity came the great booming sound of our own cannonades, the 13.5 inch and 15 inch coming into action to rescue our little ships. The crescendo of bursting and screaming shells hurtled towards us and began to bloom and burst the flowers of death, and the acrid smell of burning cordite was in the air. Our shells were leaving the questing mizzles of our guns with the speed of sound, coming out in their great arcs of high trajectory.

The range was over 20,000 yards, or approximately twelve land miles distant. The screaming, whistling crescendo of winging, bursting explosives continued for a few minutes, then there followed a sudden silence. Our enemy had had enough.

On our ships there were neither casualties nor damage, but the gallant *Cardiff* received a very severe hit from a heavy shell forrard on the bridge. The Germans had turned tail and departed over the distant horizon at the highest speed they could muster. *Cardiff* received many casualties from the hit on the bridge, and the Germans claimed to have sunk her. Not a bit of it – she came proudly in, still leading her squadron, and received a great cheer from the Battle Cruiser Force at Rosyth as she steamed past us to the dockyard for repairs and well-earned leave.

It was the last great thrill of the War, the last time the great massive guns spoke in anger.

I remember one incident connected with that trip to sea. Coming

*Right* The author as a diver, 1st Class

Victory March, July 1919. Under canvas in Hyde Park. The author is in the centre of the front rank

The plaque and crest of the HMS *Tiger,* at the church of HMS Drake, Plymouth

up on deck after dispersal from action stations, I noticed that the sea was getting up. There were grey blankets of cloud in the leaden skies and white horses rode the crest of the curling seas to gallop away beyond the horizon. While still at action stations we had a nasty accident in the after torpedo flat. It was the practice to have a 'ready use torpedo' slung overhead ready to launch into a tube after firing for a reload. On the steel decks was coconut matting on which the tubes' crew used to prevent slipping on decks and to lie and rest. The spare torpedo was suspended and held by a steel wire strop with a nose and tail rope line to steady it. Unfortunately, as the ship lurched with a shudder as a large sea hit the port quarter, the torpedo slid through the swaying strop and plunged down on top of the crew. The scene resembled a battlefield; several men had broken legs and the tail of the torpedo was smashed beyond repair.

We arrived safely back in harbour with another Action Citation to be placed on our Battle Honours on our after screen.

Just previous to this, I had spent a whole month away from the ship. I had volunteered to become a fleet ten-fathom diver. I was a very good swimmer and the thought that prompted me was an adventurous one. With the remainder of my class we were attached to the old armoured cruiser *Sutlej*, and the schoolroom was the old unprotected cruiser *Crescent*, an old squadron ship of my training days. We did most of our diving in the dockyard basin at Rosyth.

Our chief instructor was the very famous Lieutenant Cateau, the then holder of the deep water record of 34 fathoms. He did this secured to an iron chair in the murky waters of Loch Ewe in Scotland, using an ordinary rubber twill diving suit and an ordinary Seibe Gorman twin cylinder hand-operated air pump. He was a great character with a wide repertoire of fine stories. He would stop a man just as he was going to dive and tell him what had happened to so-and-so in order to illustrate a point. He was wonderful as an instruction officer.

I was only nineteen years of age and the only one selected from many volunteers in our ship. One man came from each battle cruiser to the class and I found it very thrilling.

I remember the first time I dived into the murky waters of the dockyard basin. The eerie loneliness of the descent into the dark abyss, cut off from the world above, the only friendly feeling the pulsating noise from the twin cylinder pump feeding me with life-giving air. I went down the shot rope with a prayer on my lips, then suddenly I stopped and my lead-weighted boots sank into the deep mud of the basin. I heaved a sigh of relief – I had arrived!

Now, what to do? Oh yes, wait for them to call me up! Four pulls on the breast rope which was my safety line, with telephone wires running through. Yes, there was a telephone but it seldom worked. What was it that Lieutenant Cateau had said? 'The telephone box? Forget it – except Sunday mornings. Have it polished nice and bright with your shining clean helmet on top, and one boot each side, with the brass toecaps looking like burnished gold – all for the skipper's rounds!' This was when he inspected your diving store on the upper deck.

I became calmer, there at the bottom of the dockyard basin, and even walked a few steps around my shot, which with the shot rope was my ladder to the surface. Then I felt four steady pulls on my breast rope and I knew it was time for me to rendezvous with the world of light and smiling faces. I remembered what I had to do – press in on the spigot of my outlet valve and my suit would fill with air, and I would float up the shot rope. I did this after a short time from eight fathoms deep, and slowly rose through the water. I felt the air expanding in my suit and just had the presence of mind to release the spigot of my outlet valve and so allow the surplus air to bubble away to the surface, heralding my approach to my classmates who were waiting for me to appear. Slowly from dark it gradually became light until my helmet shot above the surface of the waves. I was grateful to have arrived.

The only thing I can recall about the *Sutlej* was that when we slung our hammocks we had plenty of company: dozens of rats ran up and down our ropes like monkeys in a jungle, great black ugly things with vicious little eyes darting like sparks of fire everywhere. We were young and healthy, however, and we slept.

Towards the end of our course, Lieutenant Cateau (the pioneer of the understanding of deep water diving, who, with Professor Haldane, scientifically brought out the deep water stops to allow a diver to work off the nitrogen bubbles from his system) came into the lecture room and told us he was sorry to leave. However, HMS *Vanguard*, one of our modern battleships, had blown up at Scapa at her anchorage and sunk in 18 fathoms of water. He was to take charge of a team of divers and investigate the cause of the explosion.

Two and a half years later I was up at Scapa and still serving in

*Tiger,* when for a monthly diving exercise we went to investigate a battle practice target, an affair of wood and hessian sails. The towing spans were our objective. Just before I dived, the petty officer in charge of the diving party whispered to me that it was just about there that the *Vanguard* had blown up. The day was clear and sunny and he said to me, 'You might just see her.'

The target was moored by means of a short span of chain cable paid out astern of a fleet drifter and the long span was lying in a bight below and under the target. I went down to the bottom of the loose loop of the long span, and away out through the clear water I could just make out the wreckage of this once proud battleship. It was only a vague outline but I could guess she was a mass of twisted metal, caused no doubt by a magazine explosion.

When I got back into the boat I reported the fact and the officer said it was against orders to dive on to the wreck. We began to chat about the strange mystery of the explosions in *Natal, Princess Irene* and *Bulwark.* The cruiser *Natal* was the worst case; it happened early in the War, I believe in 1914, at Christmas, at Invergordon. Some of the officers had their wives and families billeted ashore because the ship with her squadron formed part of the Northern Patrol, Invergordon being their base.

A cinema party was in progress when the explosion occurred and in an instant the entire ship's company (less a steamboat crew doing a trip) and including about fifty civilians had lost their lives. The explosion was tremendous and parts of the ship were hurled hundreds of feet into the air. It was said that the divers were so shocked with what they saw when they investigated the wreck, that all diving was stopped. For years after the War, her bow and stern were at high tide just out of the water and two riding lights marked her grave.

The *Princess Irene* was a fleet minelayer. The same thing happened to her but at the Nore. The *Bulwark,* an older type of battleship, blew up at Sheerness. I have never heard the official view of these disasters but I think it entirely possible they were caused by saboteurs.

About this time we lost our early seaplane carrier, *Campania.* One dark night while leaving harbour she ran aground in a sickening impact on May Island and became a total wreck.

During fine weather at sea and in harbour during the evenings when the cares of the day were over, we would pace the upper deck in twos, threes, and even fours on our long after forecastle deck. We would do roughly thirty paces, turn and repeat, smoking our good plug tobacco in our pipes, often not speaking, our thoughts far away with our loved ones and many of the lads, like myself, had brothers locked in that foul battle mud on the Western Front. We would arrange our walk in the mess whilst at supper, and the talk would go like this: 'All right, Stripy, let's go on deck and dream of home.' It was very pleasant relaxation, and we would often watch the clouds sailing across the sky like frigates, and one clear night in harbour during autumn I well remember the skull of a hunter's moon turning the Forth Bridge girders into silver trellis against the sombre of the night sky.

So the New Year of 1918, with all its great hopes, was ushered in, and with the turn of the year there was a lighter feeling in the Fleet. We felt we had only to stick it out and the War would be in the bag.

Once more we went up to Scapa Flow for battle practice, and our turn came to have the concert ship alongside for entertainment. Although this was early in the year the weather was fine. After supper we came on deck to enter the concert room of this floating theatre but it was packed tight with troops, so I sat alongside our Padre who was another late arrival. He had found a seat up on deck on the hatchway combing; we felt that we were in the gods, being above and looking down on to the stage.

I remember there was an opening speech by some celebrity, an actor, and his words seemed to hang like a sad yet hopeful prayer. Then the concert started, a hush fell on the audience, and a well-known soprano started her plaintive song, 'Beside the Shalimar', one of the 'Indian Love Lyrics', her voice rising and soaring above the deep water men. We were all enthralled by the enchanting music of her voice. Outside the concert ship the sounds were stilled. The picket boats just drifted by, their crews wrapt in attention, even the screaming gulls ceased their hungry cries, and the night air was quiet so that her poignant message of love was heard for miles around.

When her song came to its tender ebb and the flood of applause had at last ceased, our Padre turned to me and said, 'That was heaven on earth, something out of this world.'

I replied, 'Yes, sir, it makes one forget the madness of War.'

I looked across the quiet waters of the Flow where the sea now seemed as serene and unruffled as a pond in an English wood. Overhead, the rising moon's golden rays were tangent to the earth, whilst in the sky a billion stars were diamonds on an ebonite backcloth, to canopy the unbelievable peace of that moment down here among the engines of war.

We now had secondary armament directors fitted aloft for our 6 inch guns, and well do I remember working with Vickers men running the electric cables through dark cylindrical cable passages deep down in the bowels of the ship, below the bilge keels. These airless and rat-infested spaces were foul places to work in; we tried air hoses, fan driven, to maintain some sort of ventilation, but with scores of men pulling the heavy rubber cored wires along the damp steel, what air we did get was soon foul and we had to work in shifts to keep alive. Believe me, we were glad to finish that job! The fourpence a day extra, 'Double bottom' money, was no compensation for the work.

Soon after this we went alongside the dockyard wall at Rosyth to have hoisted on board four 36 inch new searchlights, vastly improved controlled type of searchlights compared with our old push-around 24 inch 'Clark Chapmans'. These lights were fitted with the new Harrison lamps, wonderful illumination, said to be the best part of a million candle power and fitted with an Iris shutter, which made them extremely efficient night fighting equipment. The origin of this lamp is quite a story.

When HMAS *Sydney* shelled and drove the German commerce raider *Emden* a burning wreck on to the rocks at Cocos Island, Lieutenant Harrison the *Sydney*'s torpedo and electrical officer took a small party of 'fish men' with him to see what could be salvaged from the holocaust of the battle. They were lucky to find a good searchlight lamp inside a much damaged mounting. This of course was a piece of real luck, because our own night fighting searchlights were of a very poor quality. Taking his find on board *Sydney*, he soon discovered that it was a much superior type of lamp to our standard motor fed Clark Chapmans. He sent the lamp to HMS Vernon, the Portsmouth experimental depot, where the electrical engineers soon improved on it, and in a few months of production it was ready to be installed. In vastly superior mountings fitted with a very good parabolic mirror, and a very fast Irish shutter to blank off the glowing carbon when the light was switched off. Prior to this, the old searchlights had a piece of black painted canvas which was dropped over the front glass, a very inefficient operation. Also the new searchlights were operated by means of rod gearing for training and elevation, and the operators got on to the target by electrical instruments, a vast improvement on the old pull-push or shove method, and oceans of swear words from the Control Officer because you were waving the light beam all over the 'ogg wash' sea and sky.

But there was one bad snag in this lamp. To burn up the oxygen around the arc, to give the lamp its very white blinding light, burning methylated spirits were used, and a few of our hard cases soon got to hear of this. One night Joe Hambly, our torpedo gunner, was going the rounds when his sharp ears heard ribaldry coming from the midship pair of searchlights. He was soon up there investigating, and these men were roaring drunk on 'hooch' made from meths and burnt sugar.

Well, we placed sentries on the lamps and our medical officer discouraged anyone by mixing some chemical liquid into the methylated spirits. Of course, a few years later someone invented better carbons which did away with the use of the burning spirits.

This brings me to one more yarn. Our worst hard alcoholic was a seaman nicknamed 'General Gordon'. He with a drunkard's cunning found out that the oil lamps used for secondary lighting contained a small percentage of pure alcohol to make them burn brighter. He used to empty the lamps, fill up bottles, then drink the noxious fluid and sleep off the effects behind the warm mess deck fan shafts. He was discharged from the ship as unfit to serve afloat, and sentenced to ninety days' detention in a naval prison.

The fleet was extremely efficient now, with all the latest gun control and improved night fighting equipment.

Also about this time, that great pioneer of naval aviation, 'Rutland of Jutland', brought his ideas forward and all capital ships with centre line turrets had a wooden platform mounted on the gun barrels; usually only the midship turret was used. Of course, the idea behind these innovations was to train the guns into the wind, and with the ship steaming at the correct speed, fly off the tiny monoplanes mounted on the turret platform, and so scout ahead of the Fleet. At the start, the pilot would rev up his engine to full speed, and when he was ready to fly would drop his upraised arm and the ground crew on the turret top would release the slip holding the aeroplane, which would then fly off into the wind. Usually the plane would drop when leaving the platform and almost go into the sea, but the pilot almost always managed to keep his frail craft flying, and soon it would be winging its way over the ocean.

Quite often a pilot would say to us, 'I don't like this crate, it's too old and worn out.' Then, when flying off, he would deliberately ditch it into the sea, and then, when floating, would unhook his Lewis gun and wait for the whaler's crew to pick him up. The aircraft meanwhile would remain afloat just long enough for this operation of rescue.

The enemy was always with us in some form or another, and that winter we suffered the tragic loss off the Norwegian coast of the new destroyers *Mary Rose* and *Strongbow*; these ships had been shepherding a convoy of merchant ships when they were caught by a German cruiser. The sea was very rough at the time, which put the small destroyers at a considerable disadvantage. The cruiser was able to stand off and sink them, keeping out of range of the destroyers' torpedoes and guns. They put up a gallant fight but it was a forlorn hope; both the little ships sank under smothering shellfire. The same thing happened to the convoy. After that incident, we sent cruisers as escorts, to prevent a similar occurrence in the future.

During the very early part of 1918, when the wind still blew dismally off the sea, spindrift wet and cold and our old friends, Mother Carey's chickens, rose and dipped to kiss the cruel waves, our souls got an unexpected uplift. 'Good Alf Bentick', our skipper, cleared lower deck and told us some really excellent news. He said this windfall was due to the unrest on the Western Front. In 1917 at Verdun the French Army mutinied and the British Tommy felt terribly hurt with the way the country was treating him and his family over the cost of living, and the unfairness that munition workers had 'dry beds' and over five pounds a week earnings. Alf said, 'At last Lloyd George and his War Cabinet have awakened to the monstrous injustice to the fighting men and their families.'

We in the Fleet also felt the severe slight of the Government and the people to the needs of our families, of whom a good many had to resort to the cold charity of parish relief, or their Jack Tar husbands worked their fingers to the bone, cutting hair, 'dhobbying 'washing clothes' 'jewing' new suits, keeping other men's watches, all to help keep the hungry wolves from the door. Often a sailor's wife would have to live in one squalid room with perhaps five children to keep on her husband's very modest pay of one-and-eightpence a day. My Lord Commissioners frowned heavily on marriage for junior officers and the men. They said it was not in the best interests of the service.

Anyhow, Sir David Beatty, now C-in-C of the whole of the Grand Fleet, delegated the unrest to the good council of Admiral Jerram, Commander up at Scapa of the 3rd Battle Squadron, to investigate and recommend, and with an all Ratings and Officers Committee soon recommended a rise of a shilling per day for all ratings with a similar rise of pay for officers, and introduced an excellent scheme of helping the wives and families, including men's mothers, with the princely sum of ten shillings per week, plus two shillings per week for every child. We threw our hats in the air. Now we could afford real butter, not evil-smelling marg on our bread. I forgot to mention that *all mothers* could get five shillings per week if the sons allotted them two-and-six from their pay.

Early in February, our new Commander, Valentine Gibbs, sent for certain officers and men and asked them to volunteer for a dangerous mission which he said was secret. This mission turned out to be the daring and successful raid on Zeebrugge. I well remember two of my shipmates taking part in this raid; one was Ben Smyth, the trainer of my old gun S3, and the other, dear old Windy Turner, both very tough characters, seamen of the old school, trained in sail and steam.

The raid took place in St George's Day, 23rd April. 'Cry God for England, Harry and St George.'

We put to sea as a precaution in case any of the German heavy units came out, but as it turned out, we did not fire a shot. Our spotting top crews reported gun flashes to the south-east, and also heard the rumble of heavy gunfire, but we were not called upon to take part. We heard that Valentine Gibbs, our gallant Commander, had won a posthumous Victoria Cross. He helped to secure the gangways of the *Vindictive* alongside the mole and was killed while doing so. Ben Smyth and Windy Turner were both wounded and taken prisoner.

Then, in August 1918, influenza swept through Europe and thence to Britain; it was like a virulent plague, for it killed many thousands of people. We in the Fleet did not escape it either. All the ships' doctors and sick-bay staff, plus other helpers, worked around the clock, with patients lying everywhere. We had over two hundred cases ourselves. The worst hit was the *Princess Royal*, which could not go to sea as there were not enough fit men on their feet to man the guns, but fortunately the ailment eventually died out.

By this time we were sinking more U-boats than they were sinking our merchantmen. Along the military fronts in Europe, the Allies had gone over to the offensive and the benefit of American men and arms was being felt.

In October we went into dockyard hands for the last time during the War, and our last well-earned leave.

Soon we were back and fighting fit once more.

That month the Germans were ordered to sea to do battle with us but that was the end of a great Navy. All ships' companies mutinied and refused to take their ships to sea. They had no desire to face our great naval power. The lesson of Jutland had gone home with a vengeance.

A few days later a gallant effort was attempted by a crew of German officers, manning a large U-boat, to make a heroic attempt to get into Scapa Flow to sink some of our ships, a forlorn hope. The U-boat died in our minefields, a very noteworthy effort. That was the last sortie against our Fleet, if you can so name it. A few U-boats did remain at sea, sticking it out to the very end.

CHAPTER 9

# Armistice and the Surrender of the German Fleet

On 11th November, we were coaling ship, just 'topping up' a 400-ton job, which we did once every week, when we needed our bunkers filling. Suddenly, amidst the whirling, clanging noise of the derricks and the music of the shovels, came the clarion notes of the 'Still' on the bugle. The noise slowly died away as we saw and heard, like a veritable light from heaven, the massed band of ships' buglers sound that historic 'Cease Fire'. To me and hundreds more it was like diving into a cool pond of peace after such a long bloody struggle. As the bugle notes died away, our evening-dressed reservist leapt up to the top of the coal heap, looking for all the world like an unwashed emperor penguin, and raising his now battered topper, gracefully and with acme of elegance, gave an old world bow to the emissaries of the good news.

The time was six bells in the forenoon, 11 a.m. At first men seemed dazed and then the full impact of the news sent everyone mad with delight. I can still recall seeing 'Yank' Pester leaping on to a twenty-bag hoist and shouting to the winchman, 'Take her away, Mr Polkinhorne,' and everyone cheering furiously as he swung crazily up on to the upper deck.

We knew that the end was in sight, in fact we had known for some time, but we had also been warned that Jerry might have one last fling and that we must not let up our vigilance for one moment. The pent-up feelings of over four years of terrible war sent men into a hysteria of delight. I shall never forget it. Then the buglers sounded 'Clear Lower Deck' and we all tropped aft on to the quarter deck. We swarmed round our dear skipper, shaking him by the hand.

At last good Alf Bentick was able to make himself heard, and with tears in his eyes he thanked us for all we had done. He said, 'If

I could send you all on leave I would do so, but we must await instructions from the Admiralty.'

We shook hands all round and many sank to their knees to give thanks to the good Lord for our deliverance. Then a sheaf of signals was thrust into Captain Bentick's hands and he read out the gist of them – thanks from the King and Queen, and the Lord Commissioner of the Admiralty.

That dinner time the historic signal, 'Splice the Main Brace' was piped and each man received an extra tot of rum. This is a gift very rarely given and it came from our Sailor King, George V. The rum caterers in each mess kept that tot back for the evening celebrations.

That afternoon I went on shore to train. I was a member of the Ships' Harriers, a marathon man. We use to run seven or eight miles out to Lord Elgin's estate and back again to the local YMCA. With the remainder of the ship's team I arrived back very thirsty at the great tin huts of the YMCA, the time being roughly 4 p.m.

Back on board I witnessed the start of the festivities. It was switching on of all searchlights to the huge Fleet of ships that really started the ball rolling. Just before this we held a number of short Services of Thanksgiving, after which the officers, joined by the Padre, followed us in the celebrations.

The Americans started the firework displays and we soon joined them with bursting rockets. All over the night sky went the whirling lights. All the ships' bands piled into harbour launches and went round the Fleet, serenading the ships with all the old war songs, a crowd of sailors going along with torches to illuminate them. For the first time ever we had our upper deck lights switched on, lit by ordinary white lights, and what a welcome sight it was!

This was, indeed, a night to remember! I was amazed when I saw an American sailor climb aloft up the ship's trellis mast with a can of paraffin slung around his shoulders. Reaching the crow's nest, he proceeded to pour the paraffin all over his clothes, then with an air of nonchalance he set fire to himself. Giving a wave to the watchers below, the human torch dived fifty feet into the waters, everyone giving him a tremendous cheer. The whole harbour was now ablaze with wheeling searchlight beams. It was wonderful to watch after over four years of darkness. The wardroom bottles of whisky began to chase down the extra tot of rum and we became increasingly merry as the night wore on.

The night was dry and fine and our pale faces were showing in the light of the moon which was glowing like a brazier in the sky, and I remember walking along the after forecastle deck. The time must have been around two bells in the morning watch. It was cold under the chill glittering stars, and that old pensioner up aloft in his bright other world smiled down on the now few happy tars and I made my way to my favourite spot, the port 6 inch gun control tower, to look around the harbour and commune with the gods. The decks were wet with the dew of the herald morning, and up here surrounded by the cold steel, I pulled my 'lammy' jacket tighter around my body and lit a 'tickler'. The noise of the festivities by now had died away and I could only hear the slap of the sea and the rumble of the wind like the thunder of past events. My mind wandered back over the times of the last dreadful four years, and I recalled my dead shipmates, and hoped that they had found a billet in heaven, which they richly deserved.

Down on deck again I met a few of my pals, newly installed lamps in our upper deck lighting showing our faces pale with tiredness. When at last the harbour lights were dawning they drifted away in ones and twos and turned into their hammocks, tired out but happy. I remained a while still in a thoughtful mood, leaning on the guard rails, now smoking my pipe. All was now quiet, the hour was steeped in peace, and a cobweb dawn of a fine autumn morning was slowly filling the sky to the east, and I too turned and left.

The hands were called at the unusual time of eight in the morning but very few turned out until much later. No work was done that day, except normal watch-keeping. That evening we held a proper Church Service on the quarter deck with the Captain reading the lesson, the Padre saying prayers, and the old familiar naval hymns being sung. It was a great Service of Thanksgiving.

We received many signals from many sources, some from past officers who had fought with us at the Dogger Bank and at Jutland. The most eventful source of information was the signal from the Admiralty regarding the surrender of the German Fleet.

A few days later – I think it would be the 21st November – we put to sea for the last great drama of the war, to meet and escort in our defeated foe. This had never happened before in the history of maritime warfare – the surrender of a complete Fleet of enemy warships. It was incredible. It was the moment of truth for us, the answer to all those writers who never fought at Jutland.

We steered out past May Island in great long serried ranks to meet our late enemy. Out of the winter mist they slowly appeared. What a contrast – no longer going proudly into action, but guns trained fore and aft silent in despair. They were being led in by the Flagship of the 1st Light Cruiser Squadron, *Cardiff*. The last time we spoke about her was in our final action in the Skagerrak, with her bridge blown away by a German heavy shell. She was given the honour of leading our late enemy into captivity.

We, and the whole of the Grand Fleet, which of course included the Americans, formed two huge lanes of ships, and with our guns loaded and trained on the Germans, watched them come in. We must have looked a menacing sight. The German Fleet was led in by their Fleet flagship, *Friedrich der Grosse*. On board the *Marlborough* the low insistent roll of Drake's drum was heard, and the sound of victory echoed right down the British Fleet. It was a tremendous moment. A deep hush fell upon the British Fleet. It was a situation that had no parallel in history and it was hard to grasp that fact. When the German ships came abreast of our battle cruisers, they saluted *Lion*, Beatty's old flagship, now flying the colours of Rear-Admiral Chatfield, her flag captain at Jutland.

I had come up on deck and was standing under the guns of Q turret to watch them, and I realised how low the morale of the German Navy had fallen. Their ships' sides and structures were streaked with rust and they were no longer the smart ships they had once been at the Kiel Review early in July 1914, the occasion of the visit of Admiral Sir George Warrender, commanding the 1st Battle Squadron. It was an ignoble end to a majestic Fleet that had fought so well at Jutland. It was our *Der Tag* that the Germans had boasted so much about. Later that evening we read Beatty's famous signal, that the German ensign 'would be lowered on all ships at sunset and never hoisted again without permission of the British Commander-in-Chief'.

A few days later the German Fleet left Rosyth to be interned in Scapa Flow. We went alongside the dockyard wall and proceeded on a week's victory leave, one of the many leaves we were to have in the next twelve months.

Early in January we went up to Scapa to do duty guarding the surrendered German Fleet. While there we had a very important job to do – the only time I heard the old Nelsonian order 'Repel

Boarders'. Two more enemy ships were to be added to the Fleet at Scapa. They were the Dreadnoughts *Nassau* and *Oldenburgh*. In the original Surrender, one ship had scuttled and one was unable to steam. These two made up the full complement of ships to comply with the number required by the Armistice terms.

I was detailed as a diver, to be a member of a party of officers and men to examine the ships for damage and any other trouble that could be found. As a diver I could close valves or sluice valve doors and so on, in any flooded compartments.

Next morning we watched the two German battleships arrive and waited till the crews had left and gone on board their tramp steamers. We went alongside the *Nassau* in a Fleet drifter, carrying our diving equipment. Clambering on board we were annoyed to see the filthy condition of the battleship. It was indescribably pitiable. She looked like a floating dustbin. With the carpenters' crew I went around the watertight compartments and, of course, we were also looking for booby traps. However, we found everything correct.

I walked around the upper decks later and went into the hand-loaded 11 inch gun turrets. I could see the shells were loaded by chain purchase and then rammed home by a long-handled heavy wooden hand rammer. The rate of fire must have been very slow. Inside the guns and so on was a great deal of rust, everything appearing very neglected. We walked into the ship's galley and very soon retreated; the smell was awful, the remains of a meal many moons ago were mouldering in the huge coppers.

The Chief Carpenter asked us to help in opening the Captain's cabin. It was locked and we tried many different ways of opening it apart from blowing it open; it would not budge, neither crowbars, axes or sledge hammers making any impression on it. Finally we gave up.

All the artisans and officers left the ship and a Petty Officer, a signalman and a dozen ABs were left on board. When nightfall came the signalman went up on the bridge to watch the German tramp steamer. The petty officer in charge told us all that we must expect trouble from the Germans, so, arming ourselves with boat stretchers – great wooden staves out of our cutter lying alongside – we manned the ship's sides. Just before midnight the balloon went up – a low whistle from the bridge and a hoarse cry, 'Stand by to repel boarders!' came from the signalman. A shaft of moonlight temporarily revealed a boatload of Germans pulling with muffled oars towards our ship.

A sharp order from the petty officer in charge to 'keep quiet' and wait till he said 'Now' reached us. On came the Germans; they reached the starboard side amidships and started to climb a couple of rope ladders we had conveniently left over the ship's side for their use.

We watched them come swarming up and when they were almost level with the upper deck the petty officer yelled 'Now!' and we fell on them with our staves. A sharp struggle ensued and we knocked the Germans back into the sea with many a hearty splash as they hit the icy waters of the Flow. They cursed us in German, and in English, then cursed one another for trying it on. We could only guess that they wanted to scuttle the ship.

We kept watch all night in relays, and next morning the German tramp steamer sailed; we heard no more about it, and so ended our last encounter with the Germans.

We were now getting back to peacetime routine and the Royal Navy was gradually reorganising. We spent a lot of time on shore and we very seldom went to sea. That delightful little Scottish town of Dunfermline, with the beautiful Pittencrieff Glen, saw a lot of us. We used to travel up and down from Rosyth on the Beatty Balfour Light Railway.

On the 21st June 1919, the world was amazed at the news that the main units of the German Fleet had scuttled themselves at Scapa Flow. The Battle Squadron guarding them was at sea except for one ship doing a gunnery exercise. The Germans, who had been waiting this chance, seized the opportunity and opened up the sea cocks. The surrendered Fleet sank to the sea bed of the clear waters of the Flow in a thoroughly ignominious manner.

A little later we went up to Scapa Flow and saw the graveyards of these wrecks; most of the ships had some part of keel or upperworks sticking out of the water. Some had capsized with their bottoms showing, ugly as huge whales; others were keeled over, bilges exposed, looking like the dorsal fins of great sharks. The remainder had sunk on an even keel, straight into the silt of the sea bed, superstructures, masts and funnels sticking out of the water. Already rust was showing through. It was a grim reminder of what defeat and the demoralisation of a once great and proud Fleet could accomplish.

Some days later we steamed past the sunken ships. We were led by Sir Roger Keyes flying his flag in the new battle cruisers, the mighty *Hood*. We two capital ships were escorted by nine destroyers and we were bound for a summer cruise to the old Norse islands of the Orkneys, the birthplace of the long ships. From there we went to Nyneshasm, twenty-five miles from Stockholm, and then on to Copenhagen and thence to Norway. We were inspected by the Kings of these countries and it proved a very pleasant summer cruise, the weather being glorious. On our return we were allotted to a strange mission.

We sailed for the deep Atlantic, south-west of the Azores. Here we were to be Meteorological Ship for the R.34, the first airship to fly the Atlantic both ways. We were now captained by 'Paddy' Boyle, later to become known as Admiral of the Fleet, Lord Cork and Orrery. He meant us all to make this trip a holiday.

Arriving at our rendezvous we lazed away our time. At nine o'clock in the morning the ship would be stopped from drifting and steam to the correct allotted position, then engines would be stopped. Here we were in the deepest part of the Atlantic. The weather was perfect, the water unruffled and calm, just a great deep sea swell, making the ship move in a gentle wallow. Here we played water polo and we found ourselves swimming uphill one moment, losing sight of the goalposts, and next moment sliding down a great slope of water. It was great fun.

We had a wonderful time on that, the happiest sea trip we ever had on this wonderful ship. They were halycon days and lovely nights beneath a huge tropical moon and a blaze of stars. We would clean ship until half-past eight, then clean and go to morning divisions and prayers, then 'Pipe Down' for the day. It would be deck cricket, roller skating, deck ludo, deck quoits, hands to bathe, and water polo. In the afternoon it would be cinema in the closed-in after forecastle deck. In the evening it would be dancing on the upper deck to the music of the Marine Band, or if you preferred, you could go to a whist drive in the battery decks.

There we were alone in that vast expanse of cobalt blue sea, sending out weather reports all the time. I well remember one particular night, a night of poetical loveliness, like the front cover of a Cunard guide book. A layer of mist hung low over the sea like liquid gold and a hush lay over the gentle swell like the stillness of space beyond the rising moon, and a remark from a pal of mine made me look out to starboard. He said, 'Look you,' and pointed to a stranger from paradise – a huge blanket fish, a giant ray, was drifting by and soon was lost from sight, to leave just a phosphorescent glow in the quiet waters. It was a night to remember! The ship's string orchestra was playing some haunting melody that pulled at one's heart strings and one wished one had a sweetheart by one's side.

We left these deeps of the south Atlantic after an unforgettable time – seventeen days 'rocked in the cradle of the deep'. On our return trip we saw for the first time a giant albatross, and my chum said to me, 'Look you, mon, wing span like the bloody port yard arm.' We did not return to Rosyth but went up the Channel, first to Southend, and then to Sheerness. Here we were to prepare for the Peace Celebration in London.

There, training on the mud flats we improved our marching and achieved almost guardsman-like precision, but with a difference – we had that deep sea roll of matelots! At the end of July we all entrained for London.

Never shall I forget the Fleet under canvas in Hyde Park. What an experience – sixteen men to a great bell tent, sleeping feet to the pole. Huge marquee tents for mess rooms and canteens. The girls of the Army and Navy Canteen Board fed us, and how well they did it too! It was the greatest camp I shall ever see. People still alive will well remember the first night, and of course the free beer; the boys who got fed up with carrying it in mess utensils and rolled their own 20-gallon casks down to the tents. I went for a walk around the Park and you could smell beer miles away.

The next morning we paraded in the Park, standing eight deep ready to march off. Suddenly a swarm of WRENs descended on us like a shower of mosquitoes and, with needle and thread streaming from their mouths, proceeded to sew on to our left breasts the new Victory Medal ribbon with its colourful water wave running through it. What an evolution that was! Then, like Arabs, they silent stole away, taking up their own places in the ranks. Within ten minutes of sporting the new emblem of our victory we marched through the Park to the lilting tune of 'Colonel Bogey'. Out through the gates of Marble Arch. led by Admiral of the Fleet Earl Beatty, our David, sword in hand, so proud to lead his boys, and as a mark of honour the boys from his old flagship, *Lion*, led the way.

Of course, the Navy as the Senior Service was in the van. The whole of the Allied fighting forces were there, no one being left out. This was all 'pomp and circumstance', with pageantry at its very best, and it seemed as if the whole world stood still and paid homage and thanks to the fighting forces of the Allies.

It was a long march packed with interest, all seven exhilarating miles. The spectators were deeply moved. It has always been said that London loves a pageant, and for four long years they had been starved of the peacetime splendour. Some cheered wildly and some cried, but they all loved it.

Marching through the East End we received a wonderful welcome, people going wild with excitement. We halted somewhere close to one of the great docks, where the Cockney ladies, sleeves rolled up and arms akimbo, feathered hats tilted back, surveyed us with great smiles. When we halted they dived out with whacking great china jugs filled with beer. I saw one lad close to myself go to catch an orange thrown from an upstairs window. In doing so he accidentally tore his left bicep on his own fixed bayonet held in his right hand. Never shall I forget the rolling gait of our ranks coming down Ludgate Hill, and when we reached the Strand the sun came out, flashing brilliantly from our polished bayonets. The pavements were packed with people and the cheering which had been something out of this world suddenly died away. It seemed that we had reached a pool of silence and sorrow; a large crowd of men, women and children were standing quietly crying for all their loved ones left on the battlefields. It was a moving experience.

As we marched with the bold and the brave, wc were moving through a graveyard of grief and sorrow, sorrow of a poignancy I have never known. People were stricken with the memory of their fallen menfolk, lost on the seven seas, or killed in that bloody maelstrom on the Western Front, riddled by the stuttering machine gun bullets on the Somme, scattered by the thunder of the guns of Flanders, where their blood mingled with the flowers in a corner of a foreign field which is forever England. And these people wept for those wounded and drowned in the ugly slime of Passchendaele where giant tanks disappeared and left no trace. In sympathy the marching bands ceased to play and shuffling for the first time, we lost step, then turning I saw my comrades like myself with eyes wet with tears.

The next incident I remember was the 'great swindle'. Trust Jack to find a way out of any difficulty. We had to salute the King and Queen and other members of the Royal Family, with other crowned heads of Europe, in the grounds of Buckingham Palace. It was 'salute right and wheel left'. This was a tricky order to carry out and we wanted to do it well. Remember, King George V, besides being a full Admiral of the fleet, had also been a real sailor, serving with great distinction in the Royal Naval before ascending the throne. The Navy, swinging along eight abreast with a Western Ocean roll, fixed bayonets, rifles on the left shoulder with the right hand clasping their neighbour's empty scabbard, in this way were kept locked together as the ranks saluted right and wheeled left. They looked a magnificent sight and everyone remarked how well we marched. The great event came to an end as we swung through the massive entrance at Marble Arch into Hyde Park. Overhead the RAF planes glittered in the sky like tossed gems.

A wonderful meal awaited us in the NACB huge marquee. This dinner was given by the ladies and gentlemen of the Canteen Board; they had been saving up their money for months to do this, and at the end of the banquet we gave them a loud cheer. They wished us each to take one of the miniature flags which decorated the mess room, to keep as a souvenir of this momentous occasion, and I still have this scrap of bunting to remind me of that wonderful day.

That evening the fighting men and women of the Allies received for one night the Freedom of the City of London. Believe me, it was a marvellous night – nothing to pay – and we set about and 'painted the town red'.

Next day was one of the most momentous occasions of my life. All the officers and men who had served through the war in the Fleet were entertained to a special lunch given at Mansion House by the Lord Mayor of London. The King was represented by the Prince of Wales, now the Duke of Windsor. Never shall I forget that golden moment! The 'roll on the drums', the majestic toastmaster, very erect, standing up and pausing before addressing royalty, diplomats, and the cream of society; he rapped sharply with his mallet, then announced with great dignity, 'Your Royal Highness, my Lords, Ladies and Gentlemen, pray silence. I give you a toast – the officers and men who fought at Jutland!' We all stood to attention to the acclamation of the room and the storm of applause. Earl Beatty replied suitably and the golden moment slipped away, to be fixed forever in our memories.

EPILOGUE

# 'I Stand for the Last Time on her Quarter Deck'

Early in January 1921, we sailed back to our port, Devonport, our home base, being a West Country manned ship. The dockyard mates cheered us in back into our home port after six long years; they remembered our deeds during the war and they really gave us a welcome, as did the people of the three towns, Devonport, Stonehouse and Plymouth. In spite of the grey January morning, many thousands turned out to welcome us home; they were proud of one of Beatty's battle cruisers.

On 6th January came the parting of the ways. We paid off and our ship's band played us into the Devonport Barracks HMS Vivid. Later our Captain joined us to become the Commodore of the Depot. The *Tiger* had a long refit in the dockyard.

When she recommissioned after her long dockyard refit she was the only battle cruiser left which had fought through the 1914-18 War. I saw her again while I was on the Spring 1923 cruise while serving in HMS *Delhi*, the flagship of the 1st Light Cruiser Squadron. It was at Gibraltar; she was with her flagship, the mighty *Hood*. Both ships looked magnificent with the Mediterranean sunshine playing on their brasswork and peacetime light grey enamel paint. The *Tiger* served for a couple of years as a unit of the newly-constituted Atlantic Fleet and then became the Turret Gunnery Firing ship for the two gunnery schools, Devonport's Vivid and Portsmouth's Excellent.

Late in the year 1928 I was walking through the Devonport dockyard with a diving chum of mine. We had been out on an underwater job when my friend said, 'Look, there's the old *Tiger*. I believe she's being de-commissioned before being broken up.'

I replied, 'What a shame! I still think she's the finest battle cruiser in the world.'

He answered, 'You're probably right. The *Hood* looks very powerful but she is not as good as your old ship.'

How true his words were! The *Hood* was sunk by *Bismarck* in the Denmark Straits in May 1941 – we could have done with the mighty *Tiger* then, and I recalled by friend's misgivings of 1928. He and I walked over the *Tiger*'s gangplank; she was tied up alongside the dockyard wall in the Prince of Wales Basin. It was like walking into a tomb – utterly deserted, just a few low power lamps burning. Even the rats seemed to have learned that their home was to be desecrated and had deserted her.

The erosion of time had left its mark on this very famous battle cruiser, and her coating of paint looked like a suit of 'hand me downs', as if her wearer could not afford a new rig-out.

We walked through the mess decks past the officers' wardoom and into the after cabin flat. Here I pointed out the memento of Jutland to my friend; a polished half 12 inch German shell that had failed to explode was mounted on an ebonite plinth. We walked back along the starboard 6 inch gun deck and I stood by the gun I had served during the 1914-18 War. We continued along the upper deck aft to the quarter deck and I showed him the Battle Honours on her after screen, and we stood together and read them:

CUXHAVEN RAID, 24th December, 1914.
DOGGER BANK, 25th January, 1915.
JUTLAND, 31st May – 1st June, 1916.
KATTEGAT, 21st November, 1917.
SURRENDER OF GERMAN FLEET, November 21st, 1918.

As I saluted my old ship I lived once more through many memories of her great war work. I felt very sad and yet proud to be able to say, 'I served in this wonderful battle cruiser – John Brown's masterpiece,' and so very glad to have the chance to say goodbye in the correct Service manner.

Later she was towed away, bereft of her great guns which lay rusting without turrets on the grounds of the gun wharf. She was towed to Tyneside and there broken up for scrap iron. Many years later, in the summer of 1960, I went to a Church Service in the Naval Barracks at Devonport and stayed behind to gaze with interest at the *Tiger*'s Battle Honours and her tattered ensign which she had flown at Jutland. I also read a brass plaque to her dead and wounded.

That year a new *Tiger* was born – a brand new cruiser, probably the last big ship to be fitted with heavy guns. She now proudly wears our Battle Honours on her after screen.

And so one of Beatty's famous battle cruisers is but a name in the naval history books, a story in the Imperial War Museum at Lambeth.

How shall I remember her then? Will it be when she reappeared emerging out of that holocaust of smoking flaming death, the graveyard of the *Queen Mary*, a hurtling wraith spitting defiance with her great guns blazing forth revenge? Or shall I remember her steaming flat out, going like a bomb, a great black arrow belting through the starlit night to save the life of a valuable officer, suffering from appendicitis, the huge cresting 'V' of her bow wave creaming away in a foaming wake, phosphorescent in the silver mercury of the calm waters?

Or will it be when I first saw her on that grey October morning at Clydebank, dirty with the builders' filth, but oh! so handsome, and remember that classic observation – 'long, lean and hungry'?

Perhaps it will be that time in the summer of 1919 coming into Copenhagen, round the headland, moving through the sunlit valley of the harbour, filling the whole panorama like a great artistic canvas screen, with her light grey paint, matchless, vibrant beauty, magnificent and wonderful, awe-inspiring, and yet devastatingly menacing with her great long barrelled heavy guns.

No, I think it may be the last look – the last time I saw her, her great weapons in their mausoleum turrets trained fore and aft, silent as though in death, but oh! so triumphantly proud to have served the Royal Navy so well on its lawful occasions. Somehow as I gazed at her with the westering light fading in the autumn twilight, I recalled her gallant fight in that desperate half hour at Jutland during the 'Run to the South', with the *Indefatigable* and the *Queen Mary* both gone, and the 5th Battle Squadron only just in range of the rear German ships. This was her moment! This was the acme of her achievement! The accolade of honour ... and so, at the going down of the sun and in the morning – I will remember her!

# Index

# Index